the
writing
book

the writing book

The Missouri Group:
George Kennedy
Daryl R. Moen
Don Ranly

School of Journalism
University of Missouri at Columbia

Prentice-Hall, Inc., Englewood Cliffs, New Jersey 07632

Library of Congress Cataloging in Publication Data

Kennedy, George.

   The writing book.

   1. Journalism—Authorship.   I. Moen, Daryl R.,
II. Ranly, Don. III. Title.
PN4781.K44 1984   808'.06607   83-13909
ISBN 0-13-971754-4
ISBN 0-13-971747-1 (pbk.)

Editorial/production supervision and
   interior design: Virginia Cavanagh Neri
Cover design: George Cornell
Manufacturing buyer: Harry Baisley

Printed in the United States of America
10 9 8 7 6 5 4 3 2 1

ISBN 0-13-971754-4

ISBN 0-13-971747-1 {PBK}

Prentice-Hall International, Inc., *London*
Prentice-Hall of Australia Pty. Limited, *Sydney*
Editora Prentice-Hall do Brasil, Ltda., *Rio de Janeiro*
Prentice-Hall Canada Inc., *Toronto*
Prentice-Hall of India Private Limited, *New Delhi*
Prentice-Hall of Japan, Inc., *Tokyo*
Prentice-Hall of Southeast Asia Pte. Ltd., *Singapore*
Whitehall Books Limited, *Wellington, New Zealand*

Grateful acknowledgment is made to the following sources for permission to reprint:

Page 2, Reprinted by permission of Farrar, Straus & Giroux, Inc. Excerpt from *Coming Into the Country* by John McPhee. Copyright © 1976, 1977 by John McPhee. This material originally appeared in The New Yorker.

Page 3, reprinted by permission of the *San Jose Mercury-News.*

Pages 4-5, reprinted by permission of *The Philadelphia Inquirer.*

Page 7, reprinted by permission of the *St. Louis Post-Dispatch.*

(continued on p. 155.)

contents

9   WORDS AND WHAT THEY DO TO PEOPLE

EPILOGUE

preface

This book is based on a simple premise—that good writing is good writing, no matter what the outlet. The traditional distinctions between "newspaper" writing and "magazine" writing, between "news" writing and "feature" writing are eroding under the pressures of competition and the preferences of readers. Many of those distinctions are artificial and arbitrary. Their disappearance is overdue.

The theme of this book is that good writing, whether in newspapers, magazines, or organization publications, is clear, concise, complete, and compelling. Good writing must be based on solid reporting and must be crafted with discipline. Good writing, above all, must be accurate.

Instead of just telling you about good writing or even just showing you good writing, this book is designed to help you put principles into practice. The book begins, as good writing does, with reporting, helping you do a better job of gathering the specific, detailed, interesting information you need to write well. It stresses techniques for assuring accuracy.

The next three chapters are the heart of the book. You learn how to achieve clarity and precision, how to appeal to the senses, how to link ideas with smooth transitions. You learn how to match the pace of a story to its content. And then you begin to tie together all those skills into one of the variety of story structures. You will see how to pick and use the appropriate lead and how to get from there to an ending that does more than just stop.

Then come two chapters designed to help you apply everything that has come before. You will get help in solving the special problems of writing long articles, investigative pieces, even humor. And you will discover the applications that make this book uniquely useful to people in the fast-growing field of organization publications.

The book is unique, too, in its attention to grammar and word choice.

Grammar is basic to writing. Not every grammarian is a good writer, but every good writer understands grammar. For some who use this book, the chapter on grammar will be a review. You can refresh yourselves quickly and move on. Many other writers, however, get to college, and even through it, without grasping the basics included in this chapter. For those, time spent on the grammar section will be a wise investment.

From the nuts and bolts of grammar, we conclude with an explanation of the theory behind grammar and all good writing. Probably few journalists think of general semantics as a practical aid to their craft. The rationale for this chapter is that the opposite is true. An understanding of general semantics will help you write what you mean and mean what you write. The chapter show you why good writers choose their words with care and use them with precision. It will help you do the same.

This book alone will not make you a good writer. You will also need intelligence, commitment and a great deal of practice. But if you bring those qualities to your writing, the book will help.

George Kennedy

Daryl R. Moen

Don Ranly

the
writing
book

1

the qualities of good writing— and good writers

The writer Bil Gilbert sums up in a sentence the essence of a journalist's job: "You're telling stories to strangers." The theme of *The Writing Book* is that the best way to tell any story to any strangers is with writing that captures their attention, stimulates their imagination, appeals to their senses and satisfies their demand for information. That is true whether the story is written for a newspaper, magazine or organization publication. It is true whether the story describes last night's city council meeting, analyzes a complex social problem or sketches the personality of a new company officer.

Traditionally, there have been two kinds of writers in American journalism—those who write news and those who write features. News writers often have not regarded themselves as writers at all, but as reporters. That perception, shared by editors and journalism teachers, has encouraged an emphasis on aggressiveness, on persistence, on digging out the facts and making sense of them. Stylish prose has not been stressed. Feature writers have regarded themselves and been regarded by editors and teachers as "writers," not reporters. Feature writers have been expected to be sensitive and creative. Magazine writing, in this tradition, has been the highest form of feature writing.

This distinction between reporters and writers is disappearing. Journalism and society will be better served when it is gone. Just as subject matter rather than the size of a hole on a page should dictate the length of a story, so should subject matter rather than some artificial distinction between "news" and "features" dictate the approach to writing a story, any story.

Good writing, in a newspaper, magazine or organization publication, entertains, though it doesn't necessarily amuse. It is clear, though not necessarily simple. It is detailed, though not necessarily long. It is elegant, though not necessarily fancy.

Good writing serves the writer by luring readers, holding them and bringing them back for more. That serves the publication, too. It also serves the writer esthetically, with the satisfaction of work well done, the pleasure of worthwhile creation.

Good writing serves the reader by entertaining and informing. Here is John McPhee's description of an Alaskan inn and the couple who run it:

> The Roadhouse was a good place to stay. . . . It was run, somewhat stringently, by Carroll Close and his wife, Verna, with an unnegotiable ten-thirty curfew, and signs here and there to remind you that you were not in your own home. "Don't Touch." "NOTICE: In meeting the public the proprietors of this Roadhouse do not employ profane or obscene language. We ask you to display similar restraint while quartered here." At seven in the morning in an upstairs room, cracks in the floorboards become fumaroles of coffee, and the scent draws you down from the summit. In the kitchen, under racks of utensils, is a big wood stove, and Verna Close is sprinkling salt on its hot iron surface. She is dour, silent, stolid as a ceramic cat. She places thick slices of bread over the salt to toast. Each day, she bakes forty-six loaves of bread. Carroll Close, who is in his seventies and has been out splitting spruce, brings a load of it in and commits some to the fire. He is thin, thewy, with snowy hair and eyes that flash. With his wife, he makes and serves the standard breakfast: a mound of potatoes fried in white lard, scrambled eggs, four thick hunks of buttered toast, juice, coffee, ham, jam.

Who can read that vignette without enjoyment? Note the imagery—she is "stolid as a ceramic cat," he is "thewy, with snowy hair and eyes that flash." Cracks in the floor become "fumaroles of coffee." The curfew is "unnegotiable."

But look again and consider what you have learned in those few lines. You have come to know the proprietors of this inn, their appearance and their character. You know what constitutes a standard breakfast there, and how that breakfast is prepared. You know the house rules. McPhee has given you most of what you need to assess his judgment that this is a good place to stay.

That writing was published in a magazine, The New Yorker, and then in a book. This was published in a newspaper:

> From his post high on a knoll across the Toutle River, David Johnston had an unobstructed view of Mount St. Helens and the spot on the north flank where a bulge pushed out like a roll of flesh on a fat man.
>
> It was Sunday morning. Johnston was due for a break from the job of monitoring the volcano's vital signs. His replacement, another U.S. Geological Survey scientist, was supposed to be along shortly.

While he watched and waited, the mountain was jolted by an earthquake, one of thousands that had happened since the cone-shaped peak began stirring less than two months before.

This time when the quake hit, part of the north flank began disintegrating. There was an avalanche. Five or 10 seconds passed and then, said USGS volcanologist Pete Lipman, "The volcano spilled out its guts."

Mount St. Helens exploded with the force of a hydrogen bomb, unleashing a lateral blast from the bulge that ripped stands of Douglas fir from their roots and blew them away.

The top of the mountain lifted off, reducing the summit on the north side by more than 1,200 feet. Massive slides of mud and ice flowed down to Spirit Lake and into the Toutle River, forming a natural dam more than 14 miles long. Boulder-sized chunks of pumice hurled from the volcano's crater landed more than a mile away.

From Johnston's vantage point in a supposedly safe spot, Lipman said he undoubtedly saw a dark, cauliflower-shaped cloud moving toward him at a speed of as much as 200 mph.

Said Dr. Richard Stoiber, a Dartmouth College volcano researcher, "There was the blast, followed by the heat, followed by suffocating gases. Even if you had been standing there in an asbestos suit, you would have suffocated."

The cloud probably reached Johnston in two minutes, or less. He made a radio broadcast: "Vancouver, Vancouver, this is it!"

His body has not been found. . . .

Karen Klinger, science writer of the San Jose (Calif.) Mercury-News, reconstructed one of the most awesome and destructive natural phenomena of recent times using techniques found more often in magazines or in fiction than in deadline-pressured daily journalism.

This is narrative. It begins with a sense of foreboding and the introduction of a single, tragic figure. The volcano, as if a living thing to a geologist, is personified as a bulging fat man. The element of chance that took one man's life and spared another's is underlined. Then the pace quickens. Sentences are shorter, simpler. A graphic phrase from a scientist captures the eruption far more effectively than a scientific description could have. The imagery matches the event— "force of a hydrogen bomb," "lateral blast from the bulge that ripped" giant trees from their roots. More description of the immediate physical consequences. Then, with the dispassionate explanation of a scientist and the last words of the only witness, Klinger builds to the eloquent understatement that closes the scene.

It is a gripping story and one packed with informative detail. It is good writing.

The principles of good writing apply as well to the fastest-growing segment of American journalism, organization communication. When corporations publish magazines for their employees, when professional organizations or labor unions publish newsletters for their members, when specialists publish trade journals for readers with shared economic interests, organization communication is taking place.

The practitioners are little known to and little understood by those involved in general-interest journalism. The field is widely ignored by journalism schools.

But the skills it demands are much the same as those required on newspapers and magazines. The need for good writing is as great. The same principles of good writing apply.

In some ways, the writer for an organization publication faces problems even more difficult than those of the general-interest writer. The range of subject matter is narrower, so the writer must be even more imaginative and alert to fresh approaches. The level of knowledge of the readers usually is higher, so detail and analysis become even more important. Finally, topics are often highly specialized and technical, so clarity and precision are essential. For all those reasons, organizations, like newspapers, are putting growing emphasis on good writing.

The characteristics of good writing, for general- and special-interest publications alike, are these:

1. Clarity
2. Precision
3. Pacing
4. Transition
5. Appeal to the senses

In later chapters, you will see how to achieve those qualities in any kind of writing. For now, let's look at two samples. Both were written for newspapers and both report on catastrophes. There the similarities end. The first is the introduction to a 20,000-word account of the Three Mile Island nuclear accident. The story was reported over a 10-day period by 28 people. For the coverage of which this was the centerpiece, the Philadelphia Inquirer won a 1980 Pulitzer Prize, journalism's highest award. The second story is less than half as long as the first's introduction alone. It was reported in about half an hour and written in 10 minutes. It won no prizes.

The first:

4:07 a.m., March 28, 1979.

Two pumps fail. Nine seconds later, 69 boron rods smash down into the hot core of Unit Two, a nuclear reactor on Three Mile Island. The rods work. Fission in the reactor stops.

But it is already too late.

What will become America's worst commercial nuclear disaster has begun.

Unit Two at Three Mile Island is out of control. And no one knows. No one will know, for hours.

During the next six days, America—and the world—will watch in terror and dismay as the best minds try to prevent apocalypse. They will see scientists grappling with events they had never anticipated; federal officials frozen by indecision for days; a small, previously obscure utility company haplessly repeating like a broken record that everything is all right; and a state government struggling fruitlessly to find out what is going on and what is to be done.

What they will not see are the details behind these reactions—details more harrowing even than the general impression: Nuclear workers playing Frisbee outside a plant gate because they were locked out but not warned of the radiation beaming from the plant's walls; federal officials meeting 55 hours after the accident to be briefed, and learning to their dismay that the experts could not describe what was going on; company officials meeting behind closed doors eight days after the accident to discuss not how to get the facts out but how to keep the facts hidden; broken valves fastened together with sealing compound; a state official trying for two days to get briefed by federal officials and, when he finally heard from them, being so shocked by what they had to say that he buried his head in his hands and cried: "Oh, my God."

There were also instances when men in charge, under tremendous pressure, rose to the moment,

At 7 a.m. Wednesday, a technician in the Three Mile Island control room realized that radiation was seeping from the complex. He reached for a phone and called—not his bosses, but the state civil defense office and the federal Nuclear Regulatory Commission.

Thus, men responsible for the public interest learned of the problem before men responsible for the company's bottom line were informed.

But such moments were rare.

The story from the outside was hair-raising enough to a nation confronted by the unknown.

The story from the inside is more alarming yet.

Twenty-eight Inquirer reporters over the last 10 days have tracked down hundreds of those involved—plant workers, scientists, government and utility officials, and residents—to discover the true dimensions of the crisis at Three Mile Island.

Here is their account:

The event was unique and of historic significance. The aftermath was heavy with peril and with politics. This extended lead captures those elements, and the humanity that is another characteristic of every great story.

The second sample:

Mary Reilly and her little boys were having such a good time Saturday frolicking in the pool at their Hillside home that she asked her husband, George, to get the camera and take some movies.

When he returned, carrying the camera and their infant daughter, his wife and sons had disappeared.

Then he spotted them, on the bottom of the pool under the plastic cover that had been left stretched over the deep end.

He dived in to attempt a rescue.

It was too late. Mrs. Reilly and sons Alan, 7, and Eric, 4, were dead.

Reilly became tangled in the cover himself and came close to drowning before he freed himself.

Members of the family believe the boys may have swum under the cover and become trapped, prompting an abortive rescue attempt by their mother.

An ambulance was summoned to the Biscayne Boulevard home, but Mrs. Reilly was pronounced dead on arrival at General Hospital and resuscitation efforts on the boys failed at Valley Medical Center, where they were taken.

Mrs. Reilly was 33. Funeral arrangements are pending.

This is the tale of a tragedy told the way it happened. The idyllic scene is set. Then the husband and father returns. An instant of uncertainty precedes the discovery. The attempted rescue and its failure are told in a rush. The statement of death is flat and final. The other necessary details follow concisely.

Clarity, precision, pacing, transition, appeal to the senses—these samples and all well-written stories have those qualities in common. That is true whether the story is 200 words or 20,000, whether it is the product of minutes or weeks of work, whether the subject matter is the death of a family or a threat to the nation. Many of the same techniques can be employed, too, in telling a police story or an investigative project.

The same tradition that has separated news writing from feature writing has imposed on news writing the structure known as the inverted pyramid. The goal of this structure is to cram as many facts as possible into the top of the story, leaving detail, quotes and other non-essentials for later—if they get in at all. In the traditional form, the drowning story would have begun:

> A Hillside mother and her two young sons were drowned Saturday in the swimming pool at their home on Biscayne Boulevard, police said.
> The victims were. . . .

The inverted pyramid and the "hard" lead still have and will continue to have a place, but this kind of story is not that place. In the writing-conscious journalism that is evolving now, the traditional approach is likely to be restricted to those situations in which time or importance do not permit the more thoughtful approach to reporting and writing. The other remaining appropriate use for the inverted pyramid will be in those instances in which the news is so overwhelmingly important or fascinating that a mere recital of bare facts will catch and hold the reader. Even in those cases, however, more richly detailed and carefully crafted follow-up stories will be demanded by readers and editors alike.

Just as good writing for any outlet has common characteristics, so do good writers. A good writer is:

1. Curious
2. Widely read
3. Full of ideas
4. Knowledgeable of his or her audience

The curiosity of a writer leads in several directions. The hack is satisfied to know who and what and when. The good writer is first a good reporter, and a good reporter seeks to know how and why. He or she wants to know what people think and feel about events. Writer's curiosity prompted Cal Fussman, then of the St. Louis Post-Dispatch, to visit the players of a high school coach who was stricken by cancer. Startled by the reaction of one, he questioned another. After he had interviewed eight players, he felt justified in quoting one in his story:

"Everyone wanted to get rid of him," the player said. "But we didn't want to get rid of him this way."

The story concluded:

Marler will be rooting for his team in the stands at Kirkwood High Thursday. The Pioneers will try to win one for the coach they don't really want.

An unremarkable story is made memorable by an unexpected twist.

Hugh Mulligan of the Associated Press was curious when he learned that Pope John Paul II was saying mass at a race track during his visit to Ireland. Mulligan recalls, "The helicopter pad where John Paul II would land was framed with flowers. I asked the steward what the area normally was. 'The winner's circle,' he replied. I asked where the tote board was. He said they had built the altar up over it.

"Not only that, but the Pope put on his vestments in the jockeys' weighing-in room. The bishops vested in the paddock stables, which now had a different aroma: incense from the altar boys warming up their thuribles. The New York Daily News, which had two reporters at Galway, used my AP story under the heading: 'Pope Wins, Places and Shows.'

"Here the reporter had looked, listened, sniffed."

The good writer also reads widely. If you would write well, you must know what good writing is—the look, the sound, the feel of it. Read journalism, read fiction, read poetry.

Poetry is the most-overlooked and possibly most valuable source of guidance for writers who would perfect their craft. The best poets are the most efficient users of the language. They use words precisely, making each phrase do the work of a paragraph, creating images with a single line. Read E.E. Cummings for the discipline of his art, T.S. Eliot for imagery, John Neihardt for soaring eloquence.

The best novelists have the good reporter's eye for detail and ear for choice quotes. A good reporter who wants to be a good writer should study what those novelists do with their material. Magazine journalism long has borrowed such literary devices as the narrative, the metaphor, the internal dialogue, the vignette, the first-person observer. Newspaper journalism is now starting to do the same.

Read Hemingway for pacing, for the mastery of the simple sentence, for the expert detail. Read Faulkner for his exploration of character, for the control that saves complexity from confusion. Read John Steinbeck for dialogue, for the drama of everyday events. Read Kurt Vonnegut, Ken Kesey, Richard Brautigan, Eudora Welty, Thomas McGuane.

The best journalistic writing today may well be the best writing today. The styles and subjects vary widely, but if you look closely, you will find the same essential qualities. You will also find that all of it is based solidly on good reporting.

Read Tom Wolfe, who more than anyone else created and defines the new journalism that grafts literary technique onto in-depth reporting. Read Truman Capote, whose *In Cold Blood* was the precursor of a new genre, variously called the nonfiction novel and "faction." Read Hunter Thompson, whose bizarre imagination and irreverent viewpoint make his self-indulgent wordiness bearable. Read Elizabeth Drew and George Will, two of the most perceptive and most literate writers on politics. Read James J. Kilpatrick, who is eloquent on philosophy and country life alike. Read John McPhee and Bil Gilbert, who write about nature and sports with different styles but rare talent. Read Mike Royko, who mixes humor and outrage with unique force. Read Studs Terkel, who has mastered the art of getting ordinary people to tell their extraordinary stories in their own words.

Those writers, like all good writers, are full of ideas. Behind every good story is a good idea. And every good story is full of ideas—ideas about sources of information, ideas about questions to ask, ideas about a different kind of lead to try, ideas about how to use this literary device or that quote, ideas about transition and endings.

When the American Society of Newspaper Editors began offering an annual prize for writing, the first winner was Everett S. Allen of the New Bedford (Mass.) Standard-Times.

Allen told how, as a young reporter covering a fire, he got the idea of using an iambic line in his story. Most reporters recall iambic verse vaguely, if at all, from some survey course in poetry. Allen put it to work: "Ten pumpers roared throughout the night in Sawyer Street."

After rescuing a sea duck that had been caught in an offshore oil spill, Allen was intrigued with the idea of her struggle for survival. He wrote:

> I did not sleep that night. Several times, I went to the bedroom window, squinting futilely into the deep shadows, where Ida waged the battle that each of us must fight essentially alone. There was no sound, no movement, nothing but interminable silence. I thought of her dead, one big, funny foot outstretched awkwardly and her soft head unmoving on the wooden floor of the house, and I could neither stand the image nor put it out of my head.
>
> At daybreak, I ran out, bracing myself.
>
> Behold, she stood, the wild sea rover. Her eyes were like jewels in the fresh morning. Feet apart, chest out, and bill high, she made one demand of me—and I knew what it was. I shucked and hand-fed her a pint of quahaugs, joyous at the arrogance of her reborn appetite, unmindful of the fact that she nipped me unmercifully and unintentionally.

Ideas come from reading, from observing, from wondering, from asking about a dozen bits of new information every day, "What does that mean?"

A good writer keeps in mind, while doing the reporting and when setting out to write, what it all will mean to the audience. Everett Allen's audience lives with the sea; yours may not know that a quahaug is a clam. If you're going to communicate with somebody, though, you need to know as much as you can about who those somebodies are, what they probably already know and what they're likely to want to know.

Tom Shroder, a prize-winning writer then with the Fort Myers (Fla.) News-Press, offered some advice about readers in the pages of the Gannett company's in-house publication.

"A lot of problems in writing come from forgetting that on the other end of that copy is a real human being," he notes. "And although you might have a screaming editor to encourage you to finish writing the story, the reader doesn't have anyone to encourage him to finish reading it. So it had better be interesting."

He urges a two-step process to assure that it is. "First, you have to go through hell to know exactly what you're writing about, inside and out. Then you have to leave most of it out. . . . Just keep in mind a variation of Thoreau's great imperative: 'Summarize, summarize.' "

He concludes, "The main thing to remember here is that if a reasonable reader isn't going to wade through it, it shouldn't be there."

Many newspapers and magazines study their readers for guidance in giving readers what they want and need. National studies sponsored by the American Newspaper Publishers Association show, for example, that most newspaper readers say they want news rather than fluff. But readers define news more broadly than have many editors. This knowledge of what the readers want has led newspapers to expand coverage of consumer news, health news, economic news. Readers' desires, and competition from existing and emerging electronic media, also have generated new emphasis on coverage that is explanatory, analytical and investigative rather than superficially descriptive.

Audiences vary, of course, from city to city and from publication to publication. You'll be more successful as a writer if you take the trouble to find out as much as you can about the specific audience for which you are writing.

The one thing nearly every audience seems to have in common with nearly every editor is a desire for writing that is clear, concise, complete and compelling. The goal of this book is to help you satisfy that desire.

Instead of just telling you about good writing and instead of just showing you good writing, this book is designed to help you put into practice what you read. We begin with reporting, helping you to gather the specific, detailed, graphic information from which good writing can be crafted. We stress techniques for assuring accuracy.

The next three chapters are the heart of the book. You learn what it means to be clear and precise, what appeals to the senses, what a transition looks like. You learn how to match the pace of a story to its content. And then you begin to tie together all the skills you have been learning into one of the variety of story structures. You will see how to pick and use the appropriate lead and how to get from there to an ending that does more than just stop.

Then come two chapters that will help you apply what you have learned. You put these tools to work in writing humor, in writing the long article and in writing the investigative piece. And you see how everything that has gone before can be put to use by a writer for any organization publication. The applications make this book uniquely useful to people in that specialized field.

The book is unique, too, in its attention to grammar and word choice. Grammar is basic to writing. Not every grammarian is a good writer, but every good writer understands grammar. For some who use this book, the chapter on grammar will be a review. You can refresh yourselves quickly and move on. Many would-be journalists, however, get to college and even through it without grasping the basics included in this chapter. For them, whatever time is spent on the grammar section will be a wise investment.

The final chapter, on semantics, may hold a surprise or two. Journalists often do not think of semantics as a practical aid to their craft. The rationale for this chapter is that the opposite is true. An introduction to semantics will help you write what you mean—and mean what you write. The final chapter shows you why good writers choose their words with care and strive to be specific, graphic and concrete. It will help you do the same.

This book alone won't make you a good writer. You also need intelligence, commitment and a willingness to practice. But if you will supply those qualities, the book will help.

2

good reporting: the foundation of good writing

There are two ways to capture the detail that sets the best writing apart from the ordinary. One is recounted by a character in Evelyn Waugh's classic satire on journalism, his novel "Scoop." One reporter is describing to another the exploits of the legendary foreign correspondent Wenlock Jakes:

> Why, once Jakes went out to cover a revolution in one of the Balkan capitals. He overslept in his carriage, woke up at the wrong station, didn't know any different, got out, went straight to a hotel, and cabled off a thousand-word story about barricades in the streets, flaming churches, machine guns answering the rattle of his typewriter as he wrote, a dead child, like a broken doll, spreadeagled in the deserted roadway below his window—you know.
>
> Well, they were pretty surprised at his office, getting a story like that from the wrong country, but they trusted Jakes and splashed it in six national newspapers. That day every special in Europe got orders to rush to the new revolution. They arrived in shoals. Everything seemed quiet enough, but it was as much as their jobs were worth to say so, with Jakes filing a thousand words of blood and thunder a day. So they chimed in too. Government bonds dropped, financial panic, state of emergency declared, army mobilized, famine, mutiny—and in less than a week there was an honest to God revolution under way, just as Jakes had said. There's the power of the press for you.
>
> They gave Jakes the Nobel Peace Prize for his harrowing descriptions of the carnage—but that was colour stuff.

The honest way is more difficult. Bil Gilbert summarizes it: "Observation is the basis of everything." Legend has it that the ancient Druids forced candidates for the priesthood to study an oak tree. A failed candidate would be nailed to the tree whose details he had not captured.

Druidic discipline is not practiced in newsrooms, but the precision of observation it was intended to encourage should be. Not every good reporter is a good writer, but every good writer is, above all, a good reporter. Reporting *is* observation.

Of the qualities that distinguish good from bad writing, three depend directly on observation. They are clarity, precision and appeal to the senses. The others—pacing and transition—lend grace and power to the expression of what you have observed.

Observation is an active, not a passive, process. Clarity, precision and appeal to the senses seldom are achieved just by looking or listening. You usually have to seek out information that is not readily apparent. The reporter's main research tool is interviewing. All reporters interview, but few interview as well as they might. Fewer still get beyond the interview to other sources of information and understanding. Documents, the records of business, government and personal life, can be invaluable in answering questions and providing detail. Even the methods of social science offer help for the writer who would be a better observer.

This chapter is intended to help you become a better observer by showing you how to attain accuracy, capture the telling detail and use the tools of interviewing and research.

The best writers are the best observers.

ACCURACY

The most important part of any journalist's duty is to get the story right. Inaccuracy both misleads your reader and erodes your (and your publication's) credibility. Getting the story right means more than being sure of the correctness of spellings, of names and numbers, of quotes, although that is essential. Getting the story right also means getting the context right, being sure of the background, the atmosphere, the tone you are conveying.

Close and careful observation make possible accuracy both of detail and of context. Clear and careful writing reduce the likelihood of misunderstanding by your readers.

The importance of accuracy was dramatized in 1981 by three highly publicized controversies that generated anger and embarrassment for those involved and induced considerable soul-searching among writers and editors generally. It is probably safe to assume that they also heightened skepticism among a great many readers.

Best known of the incidents was the one in which Janet Cooke, a young Washington Post reporter, wrote such a compelling story about "Jimmy," an 8-

year-old heroin addict, that she was awarded journalism's highest honor, a Pulitzer Prize. Only after the prize was announced did editors of the Post discover that Jimmy was a figment of Cooke's imagination. Having tried and failed to find such a child, she confessed, she created one. The prize was withdrawn, and the writer was fired.

Imagination, of course, is vital to good writing. Imagination helps you find the outline of a story in a welter of facts. Imagination helps you ask the penetrating question, see the fitting simile. But imagination is no substitute for diligent, detailed reporting. And imagination run wild will lead to lies. Pete Carey, a fine and honest writer for the San Jose (Calif.) Mercury News, applies to his own work a good rule. "I try not to write what I haven't seen and heard," he says. Imagination must be harnessed to reality.

The second troubling case came to light not long after the Cooke affair. Michael Daly, a columnist for the New York Daily News, resigned after a British newspaper discovered that characters in a column Daly had written from Northern Ireland were not real. Unlike Janet Cooke, Daly insisted that his characters—whom he named and quoted—were not imaginary but were composites of several people whom he had actually seen and heard.

The composite is not new to American journalism. The technique stirred up a storm a decade earlier when Gail Sheehy published in New York magazine a widely acclaimed story about a prostitute called "Redpants." The central characters in that story, too, turned out to have been composites rather than real, a fact readers were not told.

Both Sheehy and Daly defended their work, but the device they used is indefensible in journalism. The guideline for using any literary device in journalism should be this: A device that adds information is acceptable; one that distorts facts is not.

Such techniques as the composite character, compressed time sequences and fabricated scenes or dialogue distort.

Writers are bound by the rules of the genre they choose. Writers of fiction are free to create a reality to conform to their inner vision. Writers of fact, journalists, are less free. Journalists are restricted by the rules of the craft to describing the reality they can observe. The better the writer, the greater the detail and sensitivity of the observation. But distortion of the observation or making up what you haven't observed is a violation of the rules a journalist must live by.

The case of Teresa Carpenter shows that there is ample room for dispute even about the interpretation of those rules. Carpenter was awarded the Pulitzer Prize for feature writing after it was taken away from Janet Cooke. Carpenter had written for the Village Voice three stories reconstructing the events and exploring the personalities that led to murders. Her story on the murder of political activist and former Congressman Allard Lowenstein then came under attack, which culminated in a strongly worded criticism by the National News Council. The council found fault both with her reporting and her use of literary devices that, the council charged, misled readers.

The Pulitzer board re-examined the entries and reaffirmed its award, vindicating her reporting. Still open to question, however, is her handling of the literary device known as mimesis, the reconstruction of someone's thoughts. Here is an example from her story on Dennis Sweeney, the man who killed Lowenstein:

> Sweeney was utterly alone. . . . Lowenstein, he was sure, had willed the murder of San Francisco Mayor George Moscone in 1978, as well as the 1979 DC-10 crash in Chicago. . . . The plan he devised contained a simple and chilling logic. He would confront Lowenstein and demand assurances that in the future he would leave Sweeney, his family and others alone. If he got those assurances, Sweeney intended to drive home to Oregon. . . . If not, he would have to destroy his tormentor. . . .

Such unattributed reconstructions seem to suggest that the writer had interviewed Sweeney. In fact, she had not. Nowhere does the story say she did. But the lack of attribution leaves the reader to guess at the extent of the reporting. Unclear writing, like incomplete reporting, leads to misunderstanding. Carpenter's reporting was painstaking; an explanatory phrase could have demonstrated that to her readers and to her critics.

Reconstruction of scenes or dialogue is a perfectly acceptable journalistic device. Mimesis is trickier, both because you can have only one legitimate source for a person's thought and because even that source—the thinker himself—may mislead you accidentally or on purpose. Whenever you attempt any kind of literary reconstruction, you owe it to your readers to be candid about your sources and the limitations of your reporting. If your reconstruction is second-hand—that is, if you were not present for the events you describe—you owe it to your readers to attribute quotes, descriptions or thoughts to the sources from whom you got them. Attribution can be handled gracefully; inaccuracy cannot.

The credit, or blame, for introducing to journalism such devices as the composite and reconstruction, along with the use of narrative and vignette, is usually laid on the "New Journalism" of the 1960s and '70s. That is an exaggeration, arising from the mistaken notion that the "New Journalism" was really new. In fact, the style of nonfiction writing that incorporates many of the traditional techniques of fiction is better labelled "literary journalism." It fits comfortably in what the sociologist Michael Schudson has called the "story-telling" tradition of journalism. The roots of that tradition extend back through the turn-of-the-century Pulitzer era—when it was also called "new journalism"—at least into the early 19th century and Daniel Defoe's *Journal of a Plague Year*. Some look even deeper into the past and see Thucydides as perhaps the first literary journalist.

New or old, literary journalism seeks to marry the novelist's writing techniques to careful, detailed reporting. Tom Wolfe, one of the first and best-known of the "new" literary journalists, describes the approach as simply "saturation reporting."

To do it, he says, the reporter must learn intimately the people he or she writes about. "You may have to stay with them days, weeks, even months—long enough so that you are actually there when revealing scenes take place in their lives." Alternatively, the writer may, in a shorter time, learn about the subject and earn his trust so that "he will tell you what he said or what he was thinking when a specific thing occurred."

Saturation reporting is a luxury few journalists are allowed. Careful observation, however, is a tool available to any who care enough to pick it up.

Meet Mick Jagger of the Rolling Stones, through the eyes of Eve Zibart of the Washington Post:

> Here in the poster-strewn 12th-floor office of his mid-town Manhattan record company, Jagger's studied antagonism is as impersonal and as fascinating as snake eyes.
>
> Elbows poking out, leaning slightly forward, he uses his whole body the way Barbra Streisand uses her nose. There's no way to make it seem ordinary, so he accentuates its every angularity. Bent-kneed, loose-limbed, he forces the eye to admire his self-possession; and all the while he watches, with the intimate contempt of a Toulouse-Lautrec danseuse, the effect of this provocation.
>
> A photographer arrives, and instantly Jagger is pouting. He flings himself against a blank wall, head rigid, bad shadows, mug-shot-style. He deliberately draws his face into harsh lines. Like a threat, he stares right through the camera.
>
> Jagger is wearing white socks and a joint behind his ear. White running shoes, a yellow shirt and turquoise pants with black stripes—all just loose enough to suggest that he picked them up at a secondhand store. The reverse-chic of a man who couldn't get thrown out of the Four Seasons in bathing trunks.

That is portraiture, a description of appearance that reveals the character behind it. Without answering a question or saying a word, Jagger has given away something about his habitat, his style, his attitude. He has been captured by a writer with an eye for detail and a flair for metaphor.

Instead of relying for her impressions on the questions and answers that are the meat of most interviews, Zibart used her eyes as well. She noticed Jagger's surroundings; she noticed his pose, his dress, his body language. She noticed his study of her reactions.

She helps her readers visualize him, too, with precise, almost clinical detail in the description and with the metaphors that liken Jagger's qualities to things and people already known.

With a little extra effort, you can give life to a story even when there isn't much time.

Pete Carey was called in on his day off to report on the capture of a fugitive Hell's Angels leader. Working against an early deadline, he was able to give his readers a close-up of the action:

> The stocky Perkey was arrested at 9:30 a.m. when a task force of 11 federal and state agents, acting on a tip, moved on a three-room cabin hidden in a fog-shrouded stand of redwoods on McGaffigan Mill Road near Boulder Creek.

They kicked down the door and found a shirtless Perkey struggling out of bed. A teenage girl and a woman were asleep in an adjoining bedroom. . . .

Carey was not at the scene. He did not witness the arrest. He did not see the hideout. He couldn't. The drama was over before he found out about it. Instead, he did the next best thing. He used the eyes of those who were there. By asking, as too many reporters fail to do, about the surroundings of the arrest rather than just the standard police-blotter information, he got and conveyed to his readers a sense of being there.

Hugh Mulligan, a special correspondent for the Associated Press, sums up what such writers as Carey, Jennings and Zibart are doing. They are, he says, "using all the skills of observation and emotion and imagery available to put the reader at the scene of the story." Theirs is a kind of reporting, he continues, that "means getting rid of the comfortable old cliches and replacing them, or at least recycling them, with what the reporter actually saw, heard, felt, even sniffed."

You will not attain the mastery of a Mulligan without years of honing your skills, but you can start now to use those skills.

You can:

1. Look for the significant detail.
2. Look for the revealing anecdote.
3. Look with your mind, as well as your eyes, open.
4. Prepare before you start to look.

No two snowflakes are identical, but their differences are seldom important. No two people, no two situations, no two oak trees are identical, either. Your job is to sort out the important differences.

The first step is to look closely. Suppose you are looking at a successful banker. Look at the clothes. You'd expect them to be tasteful and expensive. Do they look it? Ask where he or she buys them. (You can find out from the store how much they cost.) Look at the face. You'd expect signs of maturity, of firmness, of good living. Are his or her eyes bloodshot? That could be a sign of close study of a balance sheet or of a martini glass. Make a note to find out. Is he or she deeply tanned? The banker could be a golfer, a sailor or a sun-lamp addict. Find that out, too. How is his or her hair cut? Is it trimmed close or styled and full? That may be a clue to his or her outlook on life. Look at the hands. Are they manicured or nail-bitten? Any signs of callouses? Do you detect a slight tremble? Those are clues, too. Look at the desk, at the wall decorations, at pictures of spouse and children (or note their absence). You may find indications of importance, of ego, of outside interests, of family situations.

The next step is to sort out the significant from the trivial. Those characteristics that might be expected may yield a picture of your subject as a banker like any other. Maybe he or she is. But the characteristic that doesn't seem to fit, that surprises you, that catches your attention may be the tipoff to what sets this banker apart from the others. Don't jump to conclusions. Fortify your first impressions with all the other evidence you can find—in further observation, in interviews, in assessments from others. Then, taking the sum of what you have learned, piece together the mosaic.

The third and most difficult step is deciding what to throw away. While cherishing the significant details, you have to discard the trivial ones, lest your finished product be a catalog instead of a portrait. You learn what to keep and what to throw away only with experience, because the categories shift with the subject. Much of your choice will depend on the focus of the story. Its central characters should be as detailed as you can make them; the supporting cast can be merely sketched. The real key to executing this last step lies in deciding, once the reporting is finished, what the story is and what it isn't.

Tom Shroder of the Fort Myers (Fla.) News-Press found significance in the seemingly most ordinary of details in his lead of a story about alcoholism:

> Every Sunday at 10 a.m. sharp, the sprinklers on Dave Jones' lush front lawn are switched on by remote control. The mechanical sprinkling system has made his yard the envy of the suburban Brookline neighborhood.
>
> This Sunday, like every other Sunday in recent memory, the automatic sprinklers are proving the worth of their $5,000 price tag. The sun is already high over the Jones' flowering dogwood, but the master of the house is in no condition to tend to the lawn himself. He's stone drunk on the living-room carpet.
>
> Thirty-two is a fine age for a man. It is that golden point in time when the muscles are still firm, the mind keen and the raw edge of inexperience begins to give way to the polish of maturity. But for David Jones, 32 is the beginning of the end. . . .

Age, address and the possession of a lawn sprinkler become poignant reminders that alcoholism is not restricted to the old, the poor, the derelict. Shroder spotted the significance of the usually mundane and shared it with his readers.

Shroder chose to begin his story with the description of a scene. It is a good way to convey important information and put it in context at the same time. A similar story-telling device is the anecdote, or vignette. An anecdote is a sort of story within a story. It may help to set a scene or to reveal the character of a person or a place. It may be used as a lead or in the body of the story. You will be more successful as a writer if you succeed as a reporter in capturing the telling anecdote.

In "Scoop," Waugh reveals his view of the nature of journalism as well as the character of one reporter in an anecdote he has the reporter relate.

> On Monday afternoon I was in East Sheen breaking the news to a widow of her husband's death leap with a champion girl cyclist—the wrong widow as it turned out; the husband came back from business while I was there and cut up very nasty.
>
> Next day the Chief has me in and says, "Corker, you're off to Ishmaelia."
>
> "Out-of-town job?" I asked.
>
> "East Africa," he said, just like that. "Pack your traps."

That fictional exchange has its counterparts at the highest levels of journalism. The Wall Street Journal regularly uses anecdotes to spice up what might otherwise be dull stories, such as Lawrence Rout's survey of the field of elite magazines. He began:

> When Idi Amin fled from Uganda last year, he lost his stranglehold on a nation— and his subscription to Leaders Magazine.
> Sorry, Mr. Amin, but the magazine is sent, free, only to leaders of nations, world religions, international companies, labor organizations and institutes of learning, plus Nobel laureates and notables in the arts and sciences.
> "Amin can get a copy if he becomes chairman of a big company," suggests an unsympathetic Henry Dormann, the quarterly's publisher.

The best anecdotes, vignettes or scenes are those that add something other than entertainment, though that is desirable, too. Look for the anecdote that will tell your readers something about the subject of your story. Encourage everyone you interview to think of incidents like the Amin story.

When you hear one or see it unfold before you, try to catch exact quotes, jot down the circumstances and the names of participants.

It is fair use to boil down the anecdote to its essentials, even if some participants or some quotes must be left out. It is unfair and dishonest to distort the scene or the quotes to make the anecdote funnier or more pertinent.

The Amin anecdote plays on the widely held perception of the dictator. Tom Shroder's lead, by contrast, disturbs a commonly held perception.

There's a lesson in that for writers as well as readers. Pete Carey puts it this way, "Maintain a little distance from things. Don't bring too many preconceptions to a story."

The preconception, the stereotype, the prejudice are pieces of the mental baggage we all carry. They are probably the most serious threats to good reporting and good writing. They distort vision, leading you to see only what you expected to find, instead of what may really be in front of you. No human being can exorcise them, but every writer must try.

Though some would deny it, most writers begin reporting most stories with at least some idea of what they will find. There is nothing inherently wrong with that. In scientific research, the same sort of preconception is called the hypothesis. It is accepted as the essential starting point for any experiment. The scientific method demands that the scientist, in testing the hypothesis, look for evidence to *dis*prove it. That high standard of detachment is not always met, even in science. But it is the standard that every writer should apply to his or her work.

It's fine to begin with an idea of your likely conclusion, so long as you keep your eyes and your mind open to evidence that may suggest a different conclusion. Careful observation will turn up the evidence; an open mind will accept it.

Scientists have another trick more writers would do well to borrow. In science, it is called reviewing the literature. No reputable researcher launches a study without carefully combing the journals of the discipline to learn everything possible about the research already done, the questions left unanswered, the methods others have found useful.

Too many writers reinvent the wheel with every story. An hour spent with the clippings in your newspaper morgue or down at the public library often can save days of relearning what somebody before you has already reported. In reviewing the literature, writers, like scientists, often can improve their ideas about what questions to ask and where to look for the answers. The sections on interviewing and using documents will offer more specific suggestions.

If you prepare before you look, look with an open mind and look for the significant detail, you will find, more often than not, the material with which to write compellingly.

INTERVIEWING

When you interview someone and come away with only facts and figures in your notebook, you have done yourself a great disservice as a writer. Why? Because the interview usually offers your best chance of picking up the good quotes, the enlightening anecdotes, the bits of humanity you need to bring life to any story. The facts and figures could be, and often should be, gathered from documents, which are more reliable and less likely to impart misunderstanding than most human sources. Humanity, though, is best transmitted person-to-person.

You've already seen how Eve Zibart used an interview situation to observe as well as to question Mick Jagger. You've seen how Pete Carey used interviews to fill in the details of a story he was unable to witness personally. You can use their techniques and others to improve the yield from your interviews. Here are some tips:

1. Prepare beforehand.
2. Put your source at ease.
3. Let your source lead the way.
4. Take good notes.
5. Double-check before you leave.

Preparation

A good trial lawyer never asks a witness in the courtroom a question to which the lawyer doesn't already know the answer. The lawyer doesn't want to be surprised, so he or she does extensive research before the trial begins. A writer's life is full of surprises, but homework is no less important. Without it, you may not know what questions to ask. You may not understand the answers you get. You may even be questioning the wrong person.

When Pete Carey was assigned to fly to Guyana to cover the aftermath of the Jonestown massacre, his first stop was not the ticket agency; it was the public library. He found a book on religious cults, read it and called the author. He knew a great deal about the phenomenon he was dealing with before he left home. That's an example worth following.

Start in your own office, with clippings, reference books and interviews with knowledgeable colleagues. Find out all you can about the person you're going to be interviewing and the subjects you'll be asking about. Nothing warms a source's heart and loosens a source's tongue like the intelligent questions of a well-prepared reporter.

Usually, if you are working on a profile or an investigative piece, you will delay interviews with the central figures until you have done the rest of your reporting. That makes sense for two reasons. First, the more material—facts, anecdotes, clues to personality and character—you have gathered, the more likely it is that this key interview will be productive. Second, you may not get more than one chance at a central figure, so you will want to cover all the essential points.

Establish rapport

The first few minutes of any interview set the tone and, in most cases, determine the success. Those first minutes are best spent gaining the subject's confidence, demonstrating your knowledge and preparing the way for the more serious questions to come.

Occasionally, if you know the source to be hostile or if time is short, you will have to dispense with the preliminaries. But otherwise, begin by asking a few questions the source will be glad to answer. The questions themselves will depend on the point of the interview. For a personality profile, good starting points would be family, hobbies or a recitation of the source's rise to prominence. For a harder story, it's a good idea to start out with a few inquiries about facts you already know. That's a quick test of veracity.

If your research has turned up a flattering anecdote or a bit of esoteric information, work it into the interview early. Most people respect knowledge, and everybody responds to flattery.

Follow the source's lead

You have a number of ideas before any interview about what you want and expect to get from it. A list of questions prepared in advance is a good way to be sure you cover the ground. But many interviewers make a great mistake by sticking to their predetermined course when the interviewee suggests potentially profitable digressions. Remember that he or she may have answers for which you don't have prepared questions.

If the source wants to talk about the impact of her father's death or about the treachery of a trusted associate when you had a simple success story in mind, follow the lead.

And, when the person being interviewed heads down an interesting path, encourage the trip with nods of agreement, murmurs of sympathy, pauses to encourage elaboration. Many people, especially those who feel nervous or defensive, can't stand silence. When you just sit there after a short answer, often they will feel impelled to go on talking, adding more than they had intended.

Unless you have the self-assurance and the experience of a Mike Wallace, the soft and sympathetic approach is usually more productive than abrasiveness or overt challenges.

Write it down

Many writers like to tape-record interviews. A few try to put their sources at ease by leaving their notebooks in pocket or purse. Both approaches have drawbacks. Neither is a good substitute for taking careful and complete notes.

Tape-recording is the only way to be sure of capturing extensive quotes exactly. It also offers some protection against charges of inaccuracy or distortion. The presence of the machine may, however, inhibit sources, especially those unused to dealing with reporters. And you should never rely exclusively on a recorder. It may malfunction, leaving you with nothing. Or, at best, it will leave you with a great mass of undigested information unless you have notes to guide you to the key sections that you may want to reproduce.

If you want to tape-record an interview, be open about it. Explain its value as a protection to the person being interviewed. Set up the machine with a minimum of fuss, then proceed. Usually, the source will get used to it quickly. If he or she is skittish, it's best to forgo the recording in the interest of getting a better interview.

Sometimes, you will want to start a conversation informally, without taking notes. Often, once you and the source are talking, you can unobtrusively bring out notebook and pen to jot down an address, to preserve the spelling of a name, to catch a figure. With the barrier broken, you can usually keep taking notes.

Don't try to write down everything. Do try to get down exact quotes that may turn out to be important, anecdotes you may be able to use, and names, addresses, titles and numbers. Don't count on being able to remember them.

If you feel yourself falling behind, in danger of losing something you want to preserve, don't hesitate to buy yourself time to catch up. One way to do that is simply to ask the speaker to wait a moment. Most interviewees will be happy to do whatever is necessary to have their words captured fully. If you suspect your source is one of the exceptions to that rule, you can be a little devious. Interrupt to ask for clarification or amplification of some point. It doesn't matter much which point, because while the source is clarifying you're writing down what was said earlier.

Remember that what appears between quotation marks is supposed to be the exact words of the speaker. You'll never be able to render a quote faithfully if you haven't written it down, word for word.

Double-check

At the end of the interview, take a few minutes to sum up. Go over any tricky spellings. Recheck any mathematics or technical information. Reconfirm—if you're not afraid of alerting the source to some unwitting admission—your understanding of the central points.

Then close your notebook, turn off the tape recorder—and keep on interviewing. More often than you might think, even sophisticated sources, thinking the formal interview is over, will make revealing comments. Give them that chance. There's nothing unethical about using post-interview material, so long as you have not agreed that it is off the record.

The problem of off-the-record information is more troublesome than it needs to be. Your life will be simpler if you remember:

1. Nothing is off the record unless you agree that it is. No source should be given the right to declare unilaterally, "That's off the record."
2. Similarly, you are not bound by any "off the record" claim that is made after the fact. Don't allow a source to make a statement and then try to keep you from using it. Any agreement must be made in advance if it is to be binding.
3. "Off the record" usually means "Don't quote me." A complicated system of levels of attribution has grown up in Washington and threatens to spread. Resist it. If the source means that you can't use the information at all, make him say that. Usually, sources want to protect their identity, not their information.
4. Don't spurn off-the-record information. If the source won't give it to you under any other conditions, take it. You may be able to confirm it from sources you can identify. Often, you can go back later and persuade the original source to go on the record. In any case, it is almost always preferable to know something rather than not know it, even if you can't tell the world where you learned it.
5. It you have any doubts, be sure you and your source have the same understanding about the ground rules. Don't seek that understanding by saying, "I shouldn't use that, should I?" Be positive. Say, "I can use that so long as I don't quote you, right?" Better yet, don't bring the subject up unless the source does. If nothing is said to the contrary, everything said to a reporter is on the record.

The suggestions in this section should help you make sure that the information you get will contain the detail, the context and the humanity you need to write well.

OTHER SOURCES

Most writers for newspapers, magazines and organization publications get most of their information by interviewing. That's why the stress in this chapter is on person-to-person reporting. But too many writers fail to take advantage of the other major source of fact and detail—written records. Here are a few of the most useful documentary sources, with tips on finding and using them.

Personal records

You can find out a great deal about most people without their help or even their knowledge. You can usually learn about their marital status, occupation, property ownership, major debts, political affiliation, educational and professional background. The more prominent the person, the easier your search.

Start, as always, with the material in your reference library or morgue. Check the clippings, check *Who's Who* and the directories of bar or medical associations. Check the telephone book (for spelling of name and for address). Check the city directory (for occupation and name of spouse).

Visit the city or county tax assessor's office. There, if you have a name or, better yet, address, you can find out what real estate your subject owns, where it is and what its assessed valuation is. At the recorder of deeds office, usually in the same building, you can find out from whom that real estate was acquired and sometimes how much was paid. There you can also find out who holds the mortgage and in what amount.

In the recorder's office, you also can check marriage and divorce records, which are usually filed alphabetically by name.

The registrar of voters has records that show address, birthdate and party affiliation for all registered voters. You can even learn if your subject voted in the last election.

The state motor vehicle department will tell you who owns a vehicle for which you have the license number. Depending on the state, you may be able to get driver license and driving record information, too.

The offices of clerks of your state and federal courts have records that show whether your subject has ever been sued or tried for a crime. If you find a lawsuit, look it up. It may contain a great deal of information about finances or character.

Don't forget the most obvious. If you're writing about a prominent person, ask his or her secretary for a biographical sheet. Or ask the public relations office of the company. And colleges usually are happy to relate the exploits of distinguished alumni.

Business records

Most businesses are regulated by some government agency. Find out which agency and which records it keeps. For example, the federal Securities and Exchange Commission requires detailed records from corporations that sell stock. The state insurance division regulates insurance companies, the health department nursing homes, the public utilities commission power companies, and so on. The names of the agencies vary from state to state, as do the amounts of information required.

If you are looking at a charitable or nonprofit organization, or a person connected to one, you can even get the organization's income tax return from the Internal Revenue Service. It is called a Form 990.

Don't overlook these possibilities. The information contained in records is often more complete and more accurate than you can get in interviews. And you can always identify a documentary source in your story.

You will hardly ever build a story solely on records. They are too dry, too lacking in explanation, sometimes too confusing to be used without human sources to explain, amplify, enliven them. But relying on human sources alone may deprive you of the information a writer must have.

PUTTING IT ALL TOGETHER

Now that you've seen how important good reporting is to good writing, and now that you've picked up some guidelines and techniques for improving your reporting, it's time to see how the two really fit together. Ann Frank is a young graduate of the University of Missouri School of Journalism. She was working as a feature writer on the Fort Lauderdale (Fla.) News when she became intrigued with the tragic story of Al Perlmutter. She tells how she used imagination and persistence to uncover the details and reveal the humanity behind a court case.

"This was an enterprise piece," she recalls. "It was not assigned. I worked on it between regular assignments and on my own time until the last week."

The story of a man who wanted to be allowed to die broke not long after she arrived at the News. Her own and the other South Florida papers covered it extensively, but focused on the bare facts and the legal issue.

Ann Frank became obsessed with an unanswered question: "What color are his eyes?"

"I decided to find out," she says. She reread all the clippings, went to the library for books on death and dying. She hesitated, afraid of trying and failing, aware that others had tried and failed.

"But dammit, I wanted it so-o-o bad," she says. She got it.

"I found the name of a neighbor who'd been quoted once (all of a sentence's worth). I called her and she practically hung up on me. Then something in her voice made me drop a Yiddish word, meaning "It's a shame." She asked me to repeat myself. I did. Then she asked me if I was Jewish. I told her yes. Her tone softened a bit and I kept her talking for about 10 minutes. Useless stuff, all of it. But she hadn't hung up. I told her I might drop by the condo complex and perhaps I'd bump into her. She didn't say yes, but she didn't say no either.

"I really wasn't sure what to do. So I opted for something probably unorthodox by journalistic standards. I wrote her a letter, explaining carefully my intentions. I enclosed it with a copy of a short story I wrote back in pre-Mizzou days about a man who wanted to die very badly but everyone else did instead. I put it on her doorstep, then drove away. Next day I came back and rang the doorbell.

"I introduced myself and she stared at me through a screen door. 'You left me a package yesterday, huh?' I said yes, I had. 'So what'd you hafta go and break my heart for?' And I told her I hadn't meant to. She bit her lip, opened the screen door and invited me in.

"I spoke with her for three hours. About her, her family and finally we got around to Al. When I left, she'd given me the name of someone else to contact. (She wouldn't tell me where the kids lived or how to contact them, however.)

"And that's how it went for six weeks. Hostility, resistance. Befriend them. Get them to trust me. Their hearts bled and mine really ached. I called the lawyer but no help there.

"When I'd finished with the friends and neighbors, I hounded the lawyer. I got some stuff but nothing really worth a damn, more confirmation of information than inroads. He guarded the anonymity of Perlmutter's son and daughter with the intensity of a mother lion. I didn't have a chance.

"Next stop: the hospital. This mickey mouse routine was all too familiar. I got non-answer answers from the bureaucrats. I needed a nurse. By way of a woman I'd interviewed for a story earlier, I made contact with someone who knew someone who might be able to help me. But that nurse, who turned out to be Perlmutter's nurse (unbeknownst to us initially) hit the roof. How dare I! I got relayed lectures on medical ethics, on rights of privacy.

"I backed off, turned to reading transcripts and attending the appellate hearing.

"Then one day I got a phone call out of the blue from someone along the nurse grapevine. The nurse would talk with me. Again, from one I met and talked with another."

The rest was simple, by comparison. Then the state Supreme Court ruled that Perlmutter could die. As he neared death, Ann Frank sat down and wrote the story of his life. She wrote it in the past tense.

After the burial, the family held a news conference. Perlmutter's son told the assembled reporters. "A young woman, who I never met and who never met me, who never met my father, wrote my Dad's legacy. It's all there."

As you read it, notice the detail, notice the anecdote, notice the technical precision, and notice the understatement a writer can employ effectively when she has all the material. Notice that Ann Frank found out what color his eyes were.

> Everyone who knew him agreed, the most striking feature about Abe Perlmutter was his pale blue eyes.
> Eyes that took on a mischievous glint when he kibitzed about his adventures as a cab driver in New York City.
> Eyes that charmed strangers, family and friends.
> Eyes so expressive, his words were often unnecessary.
> During his last days, those eyes became his only real means to communicate.
> Immobilized by the crippling progression of amyotrophic lateral sclerosis (Lou Gehrig's Disease), Perlmutter lay since early May in a hospital bed at Florida Medical Center in Lauderdale Lakes.
> Ever present in his room were the nurse assigned by the hospital and the monotonous hum and whoosh of the respirator which kept him alive.

Perlmutter, who always enjoyed the company of others, became a solitary figure—his quick, lucid mind imprisoned by his deteriorating body. His condition was terminal. The respirator which forced air into his lungs only prolonged the inevitable.

The machine also robbed him of speech; he could only mouth words.

There was no hope for recovery, only a question: When would Abe Perlmutter die?

Without the respirator, physicians conjectured he would die within an hour. With the respirator, a few weeks or months—but no one was certain.

"When" became the vital question in Perlmutter's mind, as well as in the minds of his two children.

To pull the respirator cord or not? Did he have the right? Would anyone who assisted him or did not attempt to stop him be subject to prosecution by the State of Florida?

The search for answers to these questions became the subjects of a lengthy, precedent-setting court battle.

Much was written about the case of Broward County State Attorney Michael Satz vs. Perlmutter, but with all the publicity and litigation, little was known about Abe Perlmutter, the man.

Who was he? What kind of man was he? For people outside a close circle of friends and neighbors, details were sketchy.

A self-employed Brooklyn cabbie for 50 years, Perlmutter and his wife, Edna, retired to Lauderdale Lakes about six years ago. He was 73 and she was 70 when she died a few weeks after his hospitalization in early May. They are survived by a son, Jerome, who lives in a Houston suburb and a daughter, Carol Perlmutter Klaman, who lives in California; and five grandchildren, ranging in age from 13 to 23. But to the close circle of friends who knew him well, and to the strangers whose lives he touched, Abe Perlmutter was much more.

His nickname was not really Abe. Friends called him Al.

Perlmutter was neither an intellectual nor a learned man. He read paperback novels and watched television. He didn't play cards. He was not a college graduate, but was rather, explained a long-time friend, a graduate of "the school of hard knocks."

His life centered around basics—family and his work. Making a comfortable living for his family was of utmost importance. In later years, his focus turned increasingly to his grandchildren and retirement.

Al was a kibitzer by nature. A man who'd tease by interjecting into conversations witty asides or peppery one-liners.

Interspersed in his conversation, too, were a number of choice Brooklyn curse words.

He was 135 pounds of sinew and muscle tightly strung on a 5-foot-7 frame. Perlmutter had the fighting instincts of a Bantam rooster.

Friends recall that if his taxi or family car was cut off in traffic, he'd drive hard and fast, overtake the other driver and challenge him to a verbal, if not physical, confrontation.

Perlmutter always carried a wrench by his side in his cab: a defense against troublemakers.

He had his share of close calls.

The one he often recounted was the time a passenger held him up at knifepoint. Perlmutter's hand was slashed in the scuffle as the agile cabbie fended off his assailant and tried to hold onto his money. Despite his injury, Perlmutter ran after the robber, got back his money and hauled off the attacker to the police.

He was a handsome man. Thick and wavy graying-blond hair complemented a brilliant pearl white smile. He always looked at least 10 years younger than men his own age, and there wasn't a false tooth in his mouth.

Although he was a proud man, Perlmutter was not vain. He felt most at home in shorts, cutoffs or a bathing suit. He was no fashion plate. "Al didn't believe in dressing up," one friend said.

He didn't like braggarts, name-droppers or people who boasted of their wealth, but was proud of the possessions he worked long hours to obtain.

The Perlmutters' Lauderdale Lakes condominium was decorated tastefully, but simply. Perlmutter's car was immaculately clean. If he wasn't in the condominium's exercise room, he was outside polishing his car. "No one kept as clean and as shining new a car as Al Perlmutter," a neighbor related.

Perlmutter and his wife lived on a schedule. Thursday and Friday were cleaning days. Other days of the week were for cooking or shopping.

"And believe me, Edna kept such a house. It wasn't dirty. Never. Sick or not, she was climbing ladders, vacuuming and dusting," a friend marveled.

Physical fitness and proper diet were Perlmutter's obsessions. None of his friends could explain why. That was just the way Al Perlmutter was for as long as they could remember.

He gulped down vitamins. He ate dry toast, honey, bran and nuts. He never ate sugar. When the Perlmutters were invited to a friend's home, he would abstain from "noshing" with the others. "He wouldn't snack on a thing. Not a thing. Three meals a day were enough for him," one woman said.

But that's not to say his meals were spartan. On the contrary, say friends, Mrs. Perlmutter was a fantastic cook, and Perlmutter enjoyed many favorite Jewish dishes like homemade flanken and borscht. His secret was moderation.

Until his illness, Perlmutter's movements were like a boy's. "Al never got up from a chair," said a friend, "he jumped up." Paddle ball, shuffleboard, bicycle riding and calisthenics were his daily routine.

He and his wife could often be seen taking three or four walks a day around the two lakes nearby their condominium.

When they lived in New York City, Perlmutter rode an English racing bike at Coney Island.

Before his illness, he rose before dawn to conduct 6 a.m. calisthenics classes for the residents of his condominium complex.

Perlmutter excelled at all sports activities, except swimming. One friend still remembers the day he and Perlmutter's son, Jerome, teamed up against the physical fitness buff for a game of paddle ball. "Two against one and Al beat us both."

The Perlmutters greatly enjoyed their home and each other's company. They were content to eat in rather than go out to dinner; to watch television, rather than take in a show or movie.

But when they joined friends or neighbors at social activities, the Perlmutters were everyone's favorite couple.

Trim and slim, they made a handsome pair.

"Both of them were very real, warm and funny people. Edna especially. She had such a sense of humor. And what a personality he had! A charmer. He'd tell stories about the famous people who rode in his cab.

"They were a real love match, all right. Still as crazy about each other after 45-some odd years. They were always well liked," a neighbor said.

Perlmutter was a sensitive and appreciative man, too. As one friend said, "Al always returned a favor plus."

He was the type of man who'd drop what he was doing to do a good turn for another, whether he was asked to or not. Friends knew when Al Perlmutter drove them to the airport or to a doctor's appointment, they'd be on time. "Al did everything yesterday." He was a punctual man.

One woman at the condominium complex especially remembers how Perlmutter "had the knack of making you feel special." Whether he hadn't seen you for months or had just spoken with you earlier in the day, he'd give you a friendly hug or kiss.

As one neighbor said, if Perlmutter had been an eligible bachelor, many of the widows would've given chase.

The Perlmutters were happy and comfortable in their hard-earned retirement, while it lasted.

Their world began to crumble.

Two summers ago, Perlmutter went to the condominium exercise room as usual to ride a stationary bicycle and to do his workout. The seat collapsed and he fell to the exercise room floor.

It was around that time, too, that Perlmutter began noticing his body was losing its responsiveness. His muscle tone wasn't just right. At first he shrugged off the slowness in his limbs as creeping old age. But the nagging doubts persisted.

There was a numbness in his fingertips. Then in his legs. He began to lose his taste for food. And despite efforts not to, he began to limp.

He had difficulty climbing stairs or carrying packages. When a friend drove the Perlmutters to the airport to catch a plane to Houston (where Edna was scheduled for circulatory surgery), Perlmutter was unable to tote the suitcases.

Friends became concerned. Al was not the same.

Once the couple returned to Lauderdale Lakes, they decided it was time he sought medical advice. The Perlmutters went to internists and specialists who confirmed the diagnosis: Perlmutter had amyotrophic lateral sclerosis.

Tagged "Lou Gehrig's Disease" for the New York Yankee great who died from the illness, amyotrophic lateral sclerosis is a progressive, neuro-degenerative condition. The nerve cells (or neurons) for some unknown reason deteriorate, leaving the muscle without their nerve supply. As a result, there is progressive weakness and wasting of the muscles. The condition ultimately leads to death from respiratory failure.

Although the Perlmutters and their friends understood the disease at gut level, no one fully accepted it.

"How could a man like Al, the picture of health, die from such a disease?" a friend asked.

Initially there were therapy and injections to slow the progress of the disease. In his favor was his always excellent health.

As often as three times a week Perlmutter went to a Boca Raton clinic for treatments. "You'd never know there was a thing wrong with him," said a friend who drove Perlmutter. "He jumped out of the car. It seemed like it was all a mistake."

But it wasn't.

He became unsteady on his feet. Grudgingly he submitted to using a cane. He tried a walker, but the effort proved too much for his weakened arms.

"Al was a battler," a friend recalled.

If Edna needed to go somewhere, the ailing Perlmutter, steadied by his cane, maneuvered himself behind the wheel of his car and drove. He had no fear of getting into an accident. He was relying on years of driving experience to compensate for his weakened muscles, friends say.

Finally, Edna and his friends persuaded him to give up driving altogether.

The same friends rallied and did the driving, taking the couple wherever they needed to go.

One neighbor, familiar with the disease, tried to explain to Mrs. Perlmutter that her husband's illness was irreversible. That things would get progressively worse.

Edna pronounced him "a very gloomy man," thanked him for his concern and went about her day.

From a cane, Perlmutter went to a wheelchair to get around. "He'd come down and sit and watch the others play shuffleboard. He'd sit and kibitz. Talk about sports."

Despite the disease, he was never cranky or grouchy with friends. "It was not what you'd expect from a sick guy," a friend said.

Mrs. Perlmutter became very stubborn about her husband's condition.

"She did most of the lifting and putting him down, out of stubborn pride and love. He became dead weight. But she did what she had to do."

Friends divided their concern between Perlmutter's deteriorating health and Mrs. Perlmutter's frail heart.

A combination aide-housekeeper was brought in by Mrs. Perlmutter to assist her around the apartment, and with Al.

Then one day in early May, Perlmutter began struggling for breath. Mrs. Perlmutter became frightened and called the rescue squad. He was rushed to Florida Medical Center where she consented to his being connected to a respirator. Only the forced air of a machine, she was told, could keep her husband from going into respiratory failure.

A hole was cut in Perlmutter's throat, a plastic tube was inserted into the hole reaching down into the trachea. The tube was attached to a respirator which pumped air in and out of his lungs.

Because of the location of the hole in his throat, Perlmutter could no longer speak, but he could mouth words. He was very annoyed at the discomfort. He banged his hands against the intensive care unit hospital bed rails in protest and for attention. He wanted to breathe unassisted. He wanted to talk. He was frustrated.

One day, a few weeks later, Mrs. Perlmutter told a neighbor and friend she wasn't feeling very well. "It's killing me! It's killing me!" she said of her husband's hospitalization.

That evening the same friend rushed Mrs. Perlmutter to the center's emergency room. Within five hours, the friend had to place two long distance telephone calls: one to Jerome Perlmutter and one to Carol Klaman, to tell them their mother had died of a massive coronary.

But some of the Perlmutters' neighbors say it wasn't so much a heart attack as it was a broken heart that killed Edna Perlmutter.

"I went into a corner and I cried my eyes, my heart out. That poor woman. Edna. My God! Why?" said a friend upon hearing the news.

When Perlmutter was told his wife had died, he cried himself to sleep.

Terminally ill, his wife dead, his children burdened by having to fly long distances to see him regularly, Perlmutter decided to take command of his own fate.

On more than three occasions, first out of annoyance at his throat discomfort, and then with another more deliberate motive, Perlmutter pulled the respirator tube from his throat.

Alarms went off. Personnel rushed to reactivate the machine.

There are many gauges on the respirator which kept him alive. How much air his lungs could hold. The amount he inhaled and exhaled. The mixture of oxygen and air. There was a place for aeresol medications to be administered.

Routinely, Perlmutter's lungs were suctioned for accumulated fluids and phlegm which hampered his breathing.

Because of his persistent effort to disconnect his life line, Perlmutter was held at the wrists by cushioned restraints to keep him from hurting himself. This was common hospital procedure, considered necessary.

Perlmutter was allowed enough mobility in his arms to give normal movement, without allowing him to wrench the breathing apparatus from his throat.

Because he couldn't use a pencil and pad to "talk" with, a nurse constructed an alphabet board for Perlmutter to communicate with. He pointed out words, letter by letter. At one point he spelled out the words "pull the cord," to his family and to at least one physician.

Perlmutter made it clear to everyone he was not willing to live like that. He was ready to die.

His children approached their father's attorney, David Hoines, to pursue their father's request, if need be, through the courts.

While the legal battle was waged, Perlmutter spent the remaining five months of his life routinely.

He stopped trying to pull out the tube from his throat. The restraints were removed.

His hospital room, designed to accommodate two patients, was about 15 feet by 20 feet. The other unoccupied bed was used to store bed linens and towels.

Perlmutter's bed was along one wall. A window was at the foot and right of the bed. Three stories up, it overlooked a typical Florida view: plenty of puffy white clouds, blue sky and sunshine.

A little television was mounted on an extendable wing arm that could be positioned before him. It had a radio channel as well. But Perlmutter was generally disinterested, though his hearing and eyesight were unimpaired.

Nurses, each working an eight-hour shift, were assigned to Perlmutter's case. At no time was he to be left alone. His children requested that visitors be restricted to his immediate family, attorney and four couples with whom he was close.

Every two hours he was turned in one direction or another to avoid bedsores or accumulating fluids in his lungs.

Perlmutter lost his appetite for a while and was fed through a nasal-gastric tube. But he returned to eating pureed foods.

The nurses regularly combed his hair, shaved his beard, trimmed his toenails, changed his bed and bathed him. Perlmutter had lost the ability to do any of these things for himself.

But he never lost his ability to be personable.

He enjoyed having nurses or therapists chatter about tennis and other sports. Personnel not assigned to his case regularly cut short their lunch or dinner hour to stop by Al's room and say hello.

With the ingenuity of a man straining at his invalidism, Perlmutter devised a number of hand signals and eye signals to communicate with. There were signs for "I want a sip of water" or "a strawberry malted." Others included: "Move me," "Need blanket," "Hot in here," "Now it's cold," and, "Don't you know what you're doing?" At times when he was misinterpreted, he'd turn his face away in disgust at someone else's stupidity. He enjoyed teasing the personnel.

When a friend asked him how he felt, he mouthed "lousy" or "rotten."

His prized possessions in the hospital room were not the cards, letters and drawings taped to the foot of his bed, but the three sand dollars sent to him by some of his grandchildren. When someone picked them up for inspection, Al's face would tighten with concern. He didn't want the dollars to be broken. Most of his time was spent dozing from boredom or taking naps. He often got a good night's sleep of six to eight hours.

He had his favorites among the pretty nurses who he'd request to attend his needs.

Many times a nurse, not on duty, would poke a head in the door and say to Perlmutter, "Now don't you go away." He'd give the passerby a wink of an eye or a look like "You've gotta be kidding."

During his hospitalization, friends and personnel would often find Perlmutter staring at the ceiling with a faraway look.

The plaster above his head became a canvas for his thoughts.

No one knows for certain what went on in his mind. A review of his life? Maybe. Or maybe he tried to work out his feelings toward his approaching death. Denial, isolation, anger, bargaining, depression and acceptance are among a dying man's moods, experts say.

At the end, his face gaunt, his body wasted thin, Perlmutter's beautiful eyes, ever so slightly clouded, were all that greeted his visitors. They lit up at the sight of his children, grandchildren and friends. But his hands were marble cold to the touch.

Room 304 at Florida Medical Center will long be remembered as Al Perlmutter's room.

To the hospital personnel it was the scene of a specially convened court session in June, Broward Circuit Court Judge John Ferris presiding.

The room where floor nurses would bring flowers and plants abandoned by discharged patients to brighten his days.

The room which hung with a tense quiet atmosphere that made them feel helpless.

The room in which Al Perlmutter waited . . . waited . . . waited to die.

Finally, the courts granted his request.

On Wednesday, he removed the tube from his throat and the respirator was secured.

For a brief time he lived on.

He died with dignity early this morning.

3

the essence
of good writing

Like a warm apple pie cooling on a window sill, good writing attracts favorable notice. That's important whether you are writing an article for a national audience or a memo for your boss. The ability to write well for large and small audiences alike is directly related to your grasp of the fundamentals. Mastering them takes time, talent, experience, help and hard work.

After you master the fundamentals, you can then move to imagery that not only delights but informs, as this example does:

> Gaithersburg, Md.—If a rabbit left a muddy footprint on the grounds of the National Bureau of Standards, someone inside this scientific warren probably could measure the evidence and pronounce the rabbit's age, weight, sex, direction of travel and maybe even its mood.
> Measurement is the name of the game for the bureau.

Everyone is for good writing like this—it has nearly as many admirers as mom's apple pie—but not many bother to explain how to achieve it. We do, because the process of becoming a good writer begins with the basics. The characteristics of good writing are common to all media: newspaper and magazine, company report and novel. Good writing is correct, consistent, concise, clear, coherent and creative. In this chapter we will discuss the first five; creative writing techniques and their application to non-fiction writing are the subjects of the next chapter.

BE CORRECT

The primary obligation of the non-fiction writer is to be accurate. Factual accuracy comes first. Get the numbers, names and sequence of events correct. Next comes contextual accuracy. Do not present the facts in a false light. It can be inaccurate to apply comments about a general topic to a specific instance or vice versa. Recycling information from clippings without taking into account changed circumstances since the original interview or news event will inevitably lead to charges of distortion.

Once you have the facts right, say it right. Incorrect grammar hinders understanding, embarrasses the writer and frustrates many readers.

Another way to ensure accuracy is to use those literary techniques that are appropriate to non-fiction and to shun those that are not. It is appropriate to use detailed description, recreate scenes, reproduce dialogue, use a narrator to tell a story and tease the reader. It is inappropriate to create composites, for a composite is not real. It is inappropriate to use mimesis unless the person explicitly tells you what his or her thoughts were. Accuracy is the foundation of every story.

BE CONSISTENT

Consistency is a virtue in voice, person, tone and style.

Consistency in voice means that you do not switch from the active to the passive in the same sentence. When you do, it is jerky and confusing:

The speakers droned, the senators napped, but finally the bill was passed.

The first two independent clauses are active. The shift to passive in the third not only ruins the parallelism but also will force many people to reread it to make sense of it. It should be:

The speakers droned and the senators napped, but finally they awoke to pass the bill.

Switching from active to passive in midsentence is like running forward at full speed, then suddenly backing up. (After the painters finished, work was begun by the carpet layers). It can be done, but not gracefully.

Consistency of person refers to the use of personal pronouns. Most journalistic stories are written in the formal third person: "he said," "she said." A more informal tone is achieved in the second person: "You write best when you write for your readers." The most intimate form is first person: "I am writing this to help you." More than thirty years ago, Rudolf Flesch found that the use of personal words increase interest and understanding. The journalistic third person is dispassionate. It establishes a cool relationship between the writer and the reader, between the newspaper and its subscribers. Use of the first person establishes a warm relationship. National Geographic and Reader's Digest have a more intimate relationship with their readers through their frequent use of stories written in the first person.

Intra-company communications are often written in funereal tones when something chattier would be more interesting and easier to understand. But whatever perspective you assume through the personal pronoun, maintain it throughout the article.

Consistency of tone means that once you match your writing to your subject and your audience, you stay with that tone. Most popular magazines are informal; academic journals and some specialized magazines are often formal. For better or worse—and it's probably for worse—academic journals are full of ponderous words and comprehension-defying sentences. Newspapers, magazines and newsletters cannot afford to be. This book is informal. This definition of "mood" from *The Random House Dictionary* is formal and confusing:

> A set of categories for which the verb is inflected in many languages, and which is typically used to indicate the syntactic relation of the clause in which the verb occurs to other clauses in the sentences, or the attitude of the speaker toward what he is saying, as certainty or uncertainty, wish or command, emphasis or hesitancy.

If that were the tone established in this book, you would be reading something else. Formality—if not pretentiousness—also produces "aggregate limit" for "total," "commencement" for "start," "terminate" for "end" and "in consideration of" for "because." To paraphrase columnist James Kilpatrick, when the temptation arises to use uncommon words, lie down until it goes away.

And last, consistency of style means that you follow your publication's stylebook, a manual containing rules of punctuation, capitalization, abbreviations and numerals. Inconsistencies of style damage your credibility.

BE CONCISE

Concise does not just mean short. James Michener is concise at great length. His novels are welcomed into homes. Newspapers and magazines come into homes to seek an audience among consumers who are busy with children, work and play. When they pause to read a periodical, readers expect to use their time efficiently. They will not read stories that meander through thickets of verbiage. We can learn from Blaise Pascal, who wrote to a friend: "I have made this letter a little longer than usual, because I lack the time to make it shorter."

Being concise means saying what needs to be said in as few words as possible. Concise writers:

1. Use vigorous verbs. Instead of "His voice went booming through the quiet morning woods," write, "His voice boomed. . . ." Instead of "The president lowered his head and disappeared into the airplane," write, "The president ducked into the airplane."
2. Eliminate redundancies. Knowing the precise meaning of words is a start. Eliminate the echo, and you'll eliminate unnecessary words. For instance, you don't "remand back" because "remand" means "to send back." In each of these examples, the italicized word says it all: *gathered* together, close *proximity, Easter* Sunday, *consensus* of opinion, close *scrutiny,* advance *planning,* absolutely *necessary,* soothing *tranquilizer, compromise* solution, carbon *copy* and for writers, the most hideous of all, excess *verbiage.*
   Then there are the cabooses—words that hitch a ride on another: canceled *out,* continue *on,* fall *down,* gathered *together,* open *up,* rise *up,* and send *in.* Unhitch them.
3. Distill your copy. Rid it of impurities. Make every word earn its own way. When you think you are done, try shortening your copy by one-third. Paraphrase to tighten yawning quotations. Sharpen the focus.
4. Value brevity. Someone once pointed out that the Lord's Prayer contains 56 words, the Ten Commandments 297, the American Declaration of Independence, 300 and the European Common Market directive on the export of duck eggs, 26,911.

BE CLEAR

The ability to express oneself clearly is crucial in all fields of work. Of all the futurists in the country, former journalist Alvin Toffler is probably known to more people than any of the others because he can write clearly. His book, *Future Shock,* has sold more than four million copies. The same is true of Carl Sagan in astronomy, John Kenneth Galbraith in economics and Aldo Leopold in ecology.

The admonition to be clear assumes that you want to be understood. That is not true of all writers. Some lawyers, for example, often are obscure for obscurity's sake. To illustrate the lengths to which lawyers will go, someone once translated "Jack and Jill" into legal jargon. It begins:

> The party of the first part, hereinafter known as Jack, and the party of the second part, hereinafter known as Jill, ascended or caused to be ascended an elevation of undetermined height and degree of slope, hereinafter referred to as hill.

The less people have to say or want known, the more apt they are to camouflage it in obscurity. You cannot conceal ignorance in simple sentences with common words.

Clarity in writing is the result of using words precisely, being grammatically correct and relying on simplified sentences.

Understanding is the prerequisite of clarity. Before you describe to someone else an oak tree or a political convention, you must understand it yourself. Understanding requires close and critical observation. Study the veins on the oak tree's leaf. Feel the texture of the bark. Picture the root system. Find a botanist to tell you how the tree lives and why. Ask yourself the two most important questions; "Do I understand this?" "Can I explain it to my readers?" Don't be satisfied until the answer to both is yes.

Clarity is impossible without precision. A rose by any other name might smell as sweet, but call it any other name and you will misinform those who don't know any better while outraging those who do. A pin oak is not the same tree as a bur oak. The men who harvest trees can all be called loggers, but the logger who cuts them down is a faller and the logger who removes the limbs is a trimmer. A good reporter captures the differences that set one tree, one job, one idea apart from another. A good writer conveys those precise observations in words that are equally precise.

Precise description appeals to the senses. That oak tree has not just a visual appearance but also texture, aroma, weight, taste and temperature. Its impact on the senses and the emotions will differ if it towers alone on the crest of a hill, stands hidden in the middle of a climax forest or clings, gnarled and stubborn, to the crevice of a cliff.

Using precisely the right word means you understand that the thesaurus lists, not synonyms, but words that are related. Few, if any, words have a synonym. Many have first cousins. Many have a whole family tree of look-alikes, but do not be fooled. Upon closer examination, you will find significant differences. You use "claim" when your source lacks proof; you use "said" to be neutral. You use "refute" when your source has proof of error; you use "rebut" to be neutral. You use "allude" when the reference is indirect; you use "refer" when it is direct. You repair a damaged building; you rebuild one destroyed. You relinquish when you abdicate; you repeal when you abrogate. You infer, but the speaker implies. Learn the difference between forego and forgo, loathe and loath, following and after, hopeful and hopefully, aggravate and annoy.

In Mark Twain's world, the difference between the right word and almost the right word was the difference between lightning and the lightning bug. These days, the difference often is a lawsuit.

To be grammatically correct, you must find all your misplaced modifiers, negotiate agreement between your pronouns and antecedents and reel in your dangling participles. It is difficult to communicate clearly when indefinite antecedents pop up in the most unexpected places. There were red faces when these sentences appeared:

> When Stro-Wold and Dresendofer owned the boar, one could send the other a collection of semen in a thermos and the boar did not have to be transported. Although they no longer share the boar, Marion Strother said they maintain a close relationship and still exchange semen.

One man's indefinite antecedent is another's embarrassment. Send your sentences into battle in tight formation. Each word, each phrase, each clause should march in lockstep with the word it modifies.

And last, to be clear, use simplified sentences. Sentences that express a single thought are easiest to understand. So are sentences in which the verb follows the subject, although an occasional sentence inversion attracts attention. Clarity flows from short sentences—"Jesus wept"—and long sentences:

> Oil is the Zen of American enterprise: an exercise in subterranean meditation by a handful of men, baking or freezing in the middle of nowhere, working on a tower of steel that can twist a quarter of a million pounds of pipe down three miles into the earth, through clay and water and poison gas and solid rock, probing for the silent, oozing grease left by countless slug-like creatures that died eons ago in their warm and ancient seas.

That sentence is 80 words long and understandable. This one, of 46 words, is not.

> Nor is sentence combining always an option, even if we assume a plentitude of ideational content in the writer's intention, since semantic constraints governing the grammatically hierarchical arrangement of that content require that much of it occur as subordinate inclusions within the boundaries of orthographic sentences.

Roughly translated, that means (we think):

> Even if the writer has several ideas, combining sentences isn't always an option. Some of the ideas will become subordinate clauses.

People who cannot think clearly cannot write clearly. The first rays of clarity are breaking through the fog of obfuscation even in warranties and contracts. For years the nation's second-largest bank, Citibank, provided this (and more) for a loan agreement:

> In the event of default in the payment of this or any other Obligation or the performance or observance of any term or covenant contained herein or in any note or other contract or agreement evidencing or relating to any Obligation or any Collateral on the Borrower's part to be performed or observed; or the undersigned Borrower shall die; or any of the undersigned become insolvent or make an assignment for the benefit of creditors; or a petition shall be filed by or against any of the undersigned under any provision of the Bankruptcy Act; or any money, securities or property of the undersigned now or hereafter on deposit with attached or become subject to distraint proceedings or any order or process of any court; or the Bank shall deem itself to be insecure. . .

A consultant translated it into plain English. It now reads:

I'll be in default:
   1. If I don't pay an installment on time; or 2. If any other creditor tries by legal process to take any money of mine in your possession.

Words don't fail; writers do.

BE COHERENT

You achieve clarity in sentences by using words precisely, being grammatically correct and relying on simplified sentences. But being clear does not necessarily mean you will be coherent. This sentence is clear—and confusing:

> Mrs. Brady, who is expecting her first child this month, will receive her award at the annual dinner of the Council for the Advancement of Science Writing.

That Mrs. Brady is expecting her first child has nothing to do with the award. The sentence presents us with nonsequitur; it links two unrelated facts. That's why it's confusing though the main thought is presented clearly. Armed with a set of facts, writers often fail to discriminate between what is related and what isn't. This results in sentences chock full of strange bedfellows:

> Olson, who is 5'2", said the university's financial situation is grave.

Olson's physical stature makes no sense there, but does in another context:

> The small, feisty Olson demanded that the legislature allocate more money to the university.

Thus sentences must be clear *and* coherent. Weaving those sentences together into unified paragraphs and stories is your next challenge.
   You can meet that challenge by using transitions and progressing logically from thought to thought. That gives you focus. A focused story is coherent. Coherent writing makes sense. By showing relationships, transitions help the writer make sense. For instance:

> The emergence of the United States as the leading marketer of the world's cheapest fuel was engineered by the federal government.
>   Here is how it came about:
>   The government imposed price controls. . . .

The line, "Here is how it came about" moves the reader from effect to cause. This example appears in a story written by Donald L. Barlett and James B. Steele of the Philadelphia Inquirer. They sifted through 50,000 pages of documents and interviewed dozens of people before writing a seven-part series on why the government lacks an energy policy and what the effects of that are. How to make sense of all that information? Barlett and Steele's answer was to use common words and simplified sentences, define technical terms, build transitions and logically relate cause and effect. Because they achieved coherence, they won national honors for the series. More importantly, because they achieved coherence, their readers could understand a complex subject treated in depth.

If sound sentences are the foundation of writing like Barlett's and Steele's, transitions are the girders. Using a word, a phrase, a sentence, a paragraph, the writers tied their thoughts together. Coordinating conjunctions, such as "and," "but," "yet" and "or," link two ideas of equal importance. Subordinating conjunctions, such as "although," "because," "since" and "while," link lesser ideas to more important ones. Conjunctive adverbs, such as "accordingly," "consequently," "however" and "therefore," show the relationship between two sentences. Demonstrative adjectives, such as "this," "that," "these" and "those," relate people, places and things to something in the story that preceeded them.

Using these devices, Barlett and Steele marched safely through the minefield of government energy history.

> Since 1949, the federal government has quietly spent hundreds of millions of taxpayers' dollars building—and then abandoning—nearly a dozen pilot plants and experimental facilities to produce synthetic fuels.
>
> Time and again, the plants showed that it was possible to turn coal into synthetic crude oil or natural gas.
>
> And time and again, the government and its contractors in private industry walked away from the plants, always stopping short of actual commercial production.
>
> Now, under the Energy Security Act that became law in June, the government intends to distribute not just hundreds of millions, but billions of tax dollars to oil companies to construct yet more pilot synthetic fuel plants and experimental facilities to conduct yet more tests.

Because the writers clearly signaled each turn, the readers emerged unscathed from that minefield.

Not only did the writers use transitions, they drew from the repertoire of subordinating conjunctions and conjunctive adverbs to show the relationships among the facts reported. Establishing those relationships is essential to writing cohesively. When you remove the words and phrases establishing the relationships, Barlett and Steele's story is suddenly more difficult to understand. In this version, we have lined through the words that refer to previous ideas.

> ~~Since 1949,~~ the federal government has quietly spent hundreds of millions of taxpayers' dollars building—and then abandoning—nearly a dozen pilot plants and experimental facilities to produce synthetic fuels.
>
> ~~Time and again,~~ the plants showed that it was possible to turn coal into synthetic crude oil or natural gas.
>
> ~~And time and again,~~ the government and its contractors in private industry ~~walked away from the plants,~~ always stopping short of actual commercial production.

~~Now,~~ under the Energy Security Act that became law in June, the government intends to distribute ~~not just hundreds of millions, but~~ billions of tax dollars to oil companies to construct ~~yet more~~ pilot synthetic fuel plants and experimental facilities to conduct ~~yet more~~ tests.

By eliminating the words and phrases that explicitly show the relationships and the chronology, we have damaged the coherence of the passage.

The logical progression that those terms signal is also evident in other types of reporting. When you introduce two or more elements into a story, you logically explain them in the same order that you presented them. When you use a series of numbers to show comparison, you use them in the same order consistently. When you don't, you force the reader to reread them. Compare these two examples:

Twenty percent of the faculty thinks the quality of the University has declined in the last three years, according to the survey.

Fifteen percent of the instructors think quality has declined. Twenty-six percent of the professors think it has. Eighteen percent of the associate professors and seventeen percent of the assistant professors think it has declined.

Now let's arrange the teaching ranks in logical order and insert a transitional sentence (underlined) that explains what is to follow.

Twenty percent of the faculty thinks the quality of the University has declined in the last three years, according to the survey.

(The higher their rank the more likely they are to think it has declined.) Fifteen percent of the instructors, seventeen percent of the assistant professors, eighteen percent of the associates and twenty-five percent of the professors think it has declined.

Because of the sentence explaining what the numbers will show and because the ranks were presented in ascending order, the second version is clearer.

This logical progression is evident, too, in Seattle Times writer Richard Zahler's opening in the re-creation of the eruption of Mount St. Helens.

In this case, the progression is geographical. Like the sun, it moves from east to west across Washington:

In succession, its life-giving light bathed the young wheat stalks of the Palouse and the crops of the broad Columbia Basin. The sun shone on the blossoms and buds of Wenatchee's orchards, and hastened the ripening of another bountiful cherry crop in the Yakima Valley.

In all of these examples, the writers used sentence structures that expressed the thoughts in their proper relationship to each other. You use simple sentences to state one thought, compound sentences to state two or more thoughts of equal importance, complex sentences to subordinate one or more thoughts to another. As the sentence becomes more complicated, it carries more information. For instance:

Simple:
The U.S. government lacks an energy policy.

Compound:
The U.S. government lacks an energy policy, and it faces a severe shortage of petroleum by 1990.

Complex:
Because the U.S. government lacks an energy policy, it faces a severe shortage of petroleum by 1990.

With a coordinating conjunction, the compound sentence incorrectly equates cause and effect. The complex sentence subordinates cause to effect, a more logical relationship. Sentence structure is an important element of coherence. So are the others we have discussed: avoiding the nonsequitur, using transitions, showing the proper relationships between sentences and presenting information in a logical sequence. When you have mastered this, you are ready to add your fingerprint to the story.

4

applying creative writing techniques

Style is the writer's fingerprint. The richness of the detail, the quality of the simile, the ease of the transition—these are the makings of writing style. Although there are no two identical styles, all writers use the same creative writing techniques. How and when they are used determines the style. The techniques spawn Ernest Hemingway's exquisite cadences, which emerge from surprisingly simple sentences, and James Joyce's multilayered symbolism, which lurks in enormously complicated, unstructured sentences. They parade in Ernie Pyle's no-nonsense sentences, which march like the World War II infantrymen he described, and in John McPhee's leisurely detailed descriptions of everything from canoe trips to museum curators.

Creative writing techniques require better reporting. In turn, the techniques provide you with the means to show, not just tell. You can describe someone as 32; 5-feet, 8-inches; 142 pounds; with green eyes, black hair and a scar on the left cheek. Or you can draw a picture.

At 32, John Westscott looks like an all-conference guard on a high school basketball team. His 142 pounds are evenly distributed over his 5-foot, 8-inch body. He wears a 36-athletic suitcoat, and his waist is only an inch larger than when he averaged 18 points a game for Springfield High. His hair is still black and curly, but it is a couple of inches longer now; in high school he didn't let it roll over his collar. The only reason you suspect Westscott is not a high school senior is that scar on his left cheek. It curls in an "S" from just beneath his green eye to the bottom of his jaw. A fellow GI carved it there during an argument in Saigon. . . .

To create the mental picture, the writer needed more information than the bare statistical facts; like a good reporter, he probed deeper. But even the additional facts merely tell; the imagery shows. The author used a simile ("looks like an all-conference guard on a high school basketball team"), the techniques of comparison and contrast ("his waist is only an inch larger. . . . his hair is a couple of inches longer now. . . ."), surprise ("The only reason you suspect Westscott is not a high school senior. . . .") and foreshadowing (What caused the fight?).

A writer who had just read the lead to the Westscott story was asked to describe her dog without naming the breed. She replied: "He has four legs, short tan hair, pointed ears, a white patch on his chest and stands about a foot high."

"Do it again," the teacher urged, "but this time, tell us what he looks *like*."

The student thought awhile. "He looks like he ran into a closed door," she finally answered.

"Ah," another student said. "You must have a bulldog."

For that listener, the simile *explained* what the facts couldn't.

The difference between writing with and without creative writing techniques is the difference between gourmet and fast-food dining. Our audiences yearn not only for nourishment but also enjoyment. Even if we could gulp a pill instead of a filet mignon, few of us would. We savor the juices.

Winston Churchill savored good writing. Of him, President Kennedy once commented, "He mobilized the English language and sent it into battle." Churchill used rhetoric to rally a nation; journalists use it to inform, inspire, instruct, interpret and entertain. We may be writing about war; more often, we are writing about common people doing uncommon things. By using pertinent description, analogies, personification, allusions and quotations, you, like Churchill, can win readers in war and peace.

When we finish discussing the application of these literary techniques, we will turn to three devices that give writing individuality: pacing, emphasis and repetition. We will conclude with a discussion of how to handle quotations and attribution.

USE SENSORY APPEAL

Journalists, especially newspaper journalists, often get so immersed in ordinances, burglaries, collisions, politics and environmental impact statements that they neglect to use their senses. Their idea of the facts fails to extend to the ambience of the event. Your medium may be black on white, but the world you are reporting is red, blue and yellow. You must listen to speech patterns on the streets, smell victory and defeat in the statehouse, touch the hand that builds and taste the food the poor eat.

That kind of reporting and writing has only recently been welcomed back to newspapers, where dispassionate reporting became confused with colorless writing. The muckraker Lincoln Steffens tells why he left newspapers for magazines in 1901:

> Reporters were to report the news as it happened, like machines, without prejudice, color, and without style; all alike. Humor or any sign of personality in our reports was caught, rebuked, and, in time, suppressed.

Magazines benefited from that period in journalism, which lasted nearly eighty years. Now the line between newspaper and magazine writing is blurred. Good writers, working for all media, report with their senses. Their work has texture, smell and color.

Once awakened to the richness of the detail available, many writers find themselves awash in it. Of the thousands of details you have to choose from, select only those that are pertinent. Like the crow, the amateur writer clutters the nest with things that glitter. That there was a mild breeze from the south adds nothing to a report of a city council meeting, but both *what* the public says and *how* it says it does. Good writing includes reporting on one or more of the five senses: hearing, sight, smell, taste and touch. To convey that ambience, every writer needs to know how to use the tools of analogy.

HOW TO DESCRIBE

If numbers outline, analogies fill in the features. Two basic tools of analogy are similes and metaphors.

Similes compare the unfamiliar with the familiar:

> Electrons revolve around a nucleus of an atom like planets revolving around the sun.

To most readers, the solar system is known; to many, the atom is not. The comparison is not literal. In fact, its value derives from the mental images that writers evoke with comparison. When Bil Gilbert was describing the wildlife of Tasmania for Sports Illustrated readers, he wrote, "Pademelons look like miniature kangeroos, but may be windup toys from FAO Schwarz. Wombats are about the size and shape of furry medicine balls with facial expressions like those of elderly academics." Gilbert didn't say what pademelons are literally, but he tells us what they look like. The description is concise, figurative and fun. The simile plays an important part of both lines. Pademelons *look like* miniature kangaroos, and wombats have facial expressions *like* those of elderly academics. Miniature kangeroos is a concrete description; anyone who knows what a kangeroo looks like now knows what a pademelon looks like. But the reference to elderly academics is open to interpretation. If you were describing a wombat for a science class, the description might be inappropriate without additional information. The imagery permits the audience to fill in the facial expression from elderly academics they have known or can imagine.

Similes are used to say two things are *like* each other. They begin with "like" or "as:" She walked like a queen approaching her throne. She was as haughty as a queen.

Metaphors are used to say two things are the same. "My dog's a tiger," does not mean, literally, that the dog is a tiger. It means that the dog has characteristics of one. The metaphor is a splash of cold water on a hot day; it jerks the reader to attention. You can write that Ed Koch was mayor of New York, that he is a Democrat, that he is Jewish, that he talks fast, that he is bald, all of which is true. But how do you describe the essence of the man? Saul Pett, Associated Press special correspondent, put it this way: "He is seltzer with a lifetime fizz."

Like Dr. Jekyll and Mr. Hyde, metaphors have split personalities. A mixed metaphor—one that combines two or more metaphors illogically—is a monster. This letter from an applicant to a journalism graduate school is a model of inconsistent metaphors:

> I launch this missile to probe for information about your graduate program. I enclose my resume, which should indicate what caliber I carry in my holsters.
> I have toiled in the trenches for a time, and I have reached a point at which the practice of traditional journalism no longer fulfills me. I want to teach our craft, brick by brick. . . . With my desire to teach humming in my gut, I have learned from some early research that a master's is required to get a foot in the classroom door.

The writer fizzled on the launch pad, died at high noon and buried himself in the trenches under a load of bricks; soon afterward he had surgery on his gut and his smashed foot.

Mixed metaphors and cliches are not the province only of weak writers trying to hide behind ivied walls. The Associated Press moved a story with this lead:

> WASHINGTON—A Reagan administration initiative to retrain the hard-core unemployed and move them to greener job pastures has run into a wall of skepticism in the House, where one chairman says the plan smacks of the torn roots and failed promises of the old Dust Bowl days.

The hard-core unemployed, greener job pastures, walls of skepticism, torn roots, smacked plans, failed promises and Dust Bowls make strange bedfellows.

Churchill used a metaphor of the flower—consistently—when he paid tribute to the men who moved the war supplies: "Victory is the beautiful, bright colored flower. Transport is the stem without which it could never have blossomed."

When properly used, the simile and the metaphor invite us to see familiar things in unfamiliar ways and unfamiliar things in familiar ways. They do not just decorate the story; they help the reader understand the message. They are as important to a journalistic report as numbers. Hugh Mulligan, Associated Press special correspondent, told of the time that he looked out a plane window to view the aftermath of a tornado.

> As the plane lifted out over the air museum and a small air base, we could see the devastation of that tornado two weeks ago: Small planes scattered about, helicopters turned turtle, hangars without roofs, trailer trucks flipped over, a boat blown off a lawn into someone's swimming pool, railroad box cars lying on their sides along sections of broken track.
>
> "Like a tantrum in the children's playroom," said the man at my left peering over my shoulder.
>
> I thought, "Wow, what a neat simile." In the AP tornadoes always cut a swath or mowed like a giant scythe. Who is this guy? Turns out he wasn't a journalist at all. He was an osteopath on his way to a convention in Chicago.

With all the details about the devastation of the tornado, it was left to a simile to describe what it looked like.

While similes and metaphors create mental images, another kind of comparison enables journalists to explain big and small numbers. The Philadelphia Inquirer's Barlett and Steele used the technique when they reported drilling statistics:

> In Tennessee, which produced 1,512 barrels of oil a day last year—enough to keep the cars on the nation's highways running for 19 seconds—drillers averaged one exploratory well every 169 square miles.

To report that Tennessee wells produced 1,512 barrels of oil is meaningless by itself; telling how long that much oil would keep the nation's cars and trucks running makes the number understandable. Saul Pett frequently used the technique in his profile of the federal government. Pett knew the numbers associated with Uncle Sam wouldn't mean anything unless he translated them. So he used analogies:

> It was all much easier when Jefferson was president. Then the entire federal establishment, civilian and military, numbered fewer than 10,000 persons. They wouldn't fill the Pentagon today.
>
> [The federal government] owns 775,895,133 acres of land, one-third the land mass of the United States. Uncle Sam is big in real estate.

The analogy to the size of the federal government in Jefferson's time helps us understand both the rate of growth and the size of the Pentagon now. And Pett could have told us that Uncle Sam owned 776 million acres, but it wouldn't mean as much as saying it is one-third of the United States.

Another form of analogy is contrast. Similes and metaphors establish similarities. Contrast compares to establish the differences. You can sometimes tell what something is by telling what it isn't: Ronald Reagan is no Jimmy Carter. Why, Reagan doesn't even like peanuts. Contrast is also inherent in the word "than," which ought to be used often by every writer. Pett used it to put the amount of gold at Fort Knox in context:

> To tell it straight out, there are 147,342,320.272 ounces of gold at Fort Knox, more than was ever viewed by all the pharaohs of Egypt or the conquistadors of Spain, or the Hunts of Texas.

Contrast is used to convey ideas, too. Describing unprincipled football coaches, sportswriter Jim Murray of the Los Angeles Times writes:

> They talk of "character," but they suit up pool-hall thugs, illiterates and guys they have to hide coeds from.

Murray contrasts the word with the deed. Pett uses contrast, too, to show the two sides of Uncle Sam:

> The federal government is ridiculed easily for its bureaucratic excesses, its stifling regulations, its intrusive Big Brotherism. But against that, one needs to recall it was the federal government, not the states or private industry or private charity or the free marketplace, that sustained the country in the Great Depression and saved it from revolution. It was the federal government that ended slavery in the South and had to come back 100 years later with "swarms of officers" to make that liberation real.

For writers who paint word pictures, analogy and contrast are the primary colors.

PERSONIFICATION

Personification is often the application of an extended metaphor. Animals, inanimate objects and abstractions are given human characteristics. The technique is used daily in weather reports (Mother Nature) and often in describing natural disasters. Throughout his award-winning story, Richard Zahler of the Seattle Times wrote of Mount St. Helens as a person: ". . . for the volcano in the past seven weeks had awakened from a century and a half of slumber. . . . Pressure built. Trying to accommodate that force, the mountain stretched and reshaped itself." Referring to the sale of the Delta Democrat Times, essayist Paul Greenberg wrote in the Pine Bluff, Ark., Commercial that "for four decades and more it was a voice of reason, character, and Southern courage." Abstractions are personified in uses such as "Time marches on" and "Truth does not blush." Reporters write about the "political arm" of institutions and refer to campaigns as "horse races."

Those cliches are not the only problem posed by use of personification. Sometimes we say more than we intend to. When we report, "The slippery highway caused the accident," we are neither thinking nor writing clearly. Drivers cause accidents; highway conditions contribute to them. As with all other devices, personification must be used judiciously.

ALLUSIONS

Allusion is another literary shortcut. It permits you to compare two things, people, places or events in few words. Sadaharu Oh has been referred to as the "Japanese Babe Ruth." That's shorthand for saying that Oh is the leading home run hitter. The success of the allusion depends on whether the reader knows or can determine from the context what the meaning is. Saul Pett writes:

> It is one of the ironies of history that a nation born of a deep revulsion for large, overbearing government is itself complaining, from sea to shining sea, about large, overbearing government.

He is using an allusion, "from sea to shining sea," that is well-known to Americans. When Paul Greenberg wrote of 70-year-old Orval Faubus, the man who, as governor of Arkansas, forced the federal government to use troops to enforce equal rights for blacks, he used an allusion to a legal standard: "he was scarcely a clear and present danger now." Many of his readers probably did not recognize the line as a famous legal test, but it works even for those who didn't.

Bil Gilbert used C.S. Lewis as a touchstone throughout his story about his trip to Tasmania. Anticipating that many readers would not know who Lewis was, he opened his article by identifying him as an English naturalist philosopher and novelist. Even with that help, when Gilbert later links bandicoots to Lewis, the allusion must fail for those who have not read him: "When pursued (bandicoots) hop about as if on pogo sticks, and they probably retire to C.S. Lewis' Narnia during the day." Some readers are challenged by such allusions and look them up; others are irritated by them. As always, writers must know their audience.

APT QUOTATIONS

Writers who read are better writers. And writers who jot down lines that make a point concisely, that carry a phrase well turned, are the writers who turn up with apt quotations. Bartlett's *Familiar Quotations* and *The Oxford Dictionary of Quotations* don't have compelling story lines, but they are mandatory reading. The influence of Bartlett is evident in Churchill's rhetoric. Almost 30 years before Churchill told the House of Commons, "I have nothing to offer but blood, toil, tears, and sweat," the Italian general Giuseppe Garibaldi wrote, "I offer neither pay, not quarters, nor provisions; I offer hunger, thirst, forced marches, battles and death." By his own testimony, Churchill read Bartlett's. He borrowed and improved the thoughts he found in it. Churchill loved and used the language as he did his troops.

Quotations are used to support arguments because of their dazzling syntax or for their historical context. Pett used a quote from James Madison, the fourth U.S. president, to set the theme of his article on the federal bureaucracy:

> In designing a government, James Madison said, "the great difficulty is this: you must first enable the government to control the governed and, in the next place, oblige it to govern itself." Has it?

Like Grantland Rice and Red Smith before him, sports essayist Thomas Boswell of The Washington Post shows evidence of culture and education in his writing, not to look down on his readers but to enrich them. In a prize-winning essay about athletes at the end of their careers, Boswell quotes Emily Dickinson ("I like the look of Agony because I know it's true") and John Keats ("vale of soul-making"). As he concludes, he alludes to both Dickinson and Keats:

> Look below the Yankee dollar signs and New York headlines. This is a team familiar with the look of Agony. Its players have been forced to look in the mirror. For most, their baseball world long ago became a vale of soul-making.

As with any literary device, you should not use quotations as a crutch. Use them too often and your readers will react as Emerson did, when he said, "I hate quotations. Tell me what you know."

PACING, EMPHASIS AND REPETITION

How writers use pacing, emphasis and repetition determines the personality of their writing. The three devices are evident in the fingerprints of each successful writer.

Pacing

In writing, as in art, architecture and music, form follows content. That means that the pacing of the sentences should be consistent with the subject matter. Generally, longer sentences are appropriate for more leisurely and serious topics. They slow down the reader. Short sentences convey action or tenseness. Pacing serves the same purpose as the musical score of a movie. When the scene is romantic, the music flows by like a stream. When the killer stalks his prey, the music pulses on adrenalin. When the killer strikes, the music builds to a crescendo of booming timpani and clashes of cymbals.

The story began slowly when a reporter for the Nashville Tennessean recounted how a maid had murdered a woman she had worked with for more than 50 years. Nine of the first ten sentences are between 15 and 37 words. One is five. In that sentence the writer reports, "The mistress slapped the maid." The average sentence length in the story is 29 words. But when the writer is describing the fight and murder, the sentences range between five and 14 words:

> Suddenly, consumed in anger, Alberta pushed the older woman to the floor.
> Realizing she may have hurt Miss Sadi, Alberta tried to step back. The old woman reached up and backhanded the maid across the face.
> Dazed, the maid lunged for the pistol beneath the pillow on the bed.
> "I'll end it all," she thought, as she pointed the weapon and pulled the trigger.
> The bullet struck the old woman in the head. She made a grunting sound, and the maid realized she needed to shoot again.
> She fired a second shot.

Stories on subjects ranging from murders to emotional debates to athletic competition are served by short sentences at key moments. They add a breathless quality.

Properly constructed, long sentences can too. Saul Pett opened his profile of New York Mayor Ed Koch with a 65-word sentence:

> He is the freshest thing to blossom in New York since chopped liver, a mixed metaphor of a politician, the antithesis of the packaged leader, irrepressible, candid, impolitic, spontaneous, funny, feisty, independent, uncowed by voter blocs, unsexy, unhandsome, unfashionable and altogether charismatic, a man oddly at peace with himself in an unpeaceful place, a mayor who presides over the country's largest Babel with unseemly joy.

If it leaves the readers breathless, it is supposed to. Pett was showing Koch at breakneck speed. This long sentence, which actually is an accumulation of short ones, carries the message in form as well as content.

Manipulating sentence length, then, helps you to establish the appropriate pace for your story. By coupling changing sentence lengths with a variety of sentence openings, you can avoid boring the reader. Consider the openings in the following excerpt:

> Head Start is housed in a ramshackle quarters on Fourth Street. The local center delivers a variety of services to its 20 preschoolers. The three teachers give them speech therapy, pre-reading instructions and two balanced meals. The most important thing they give the students is love.

If you read the paragraph aloud, your ear will detect the monotonous evenness of the cadence. By varying the openings and the sentence length, this writer has added pacing:

> Housed in a ramshackle quarters on Fourth Street, Head Start delivers a variety of services to its 20 preschoolers. The three teachers dish out speech therapy, pre-reading instruction and two balanced meals. And love.

Instead of four sentences with 46 words, there are now three with 34; instead of sentences ranging from 10 to 13 words, they now range from two to 19; instead of having three sentences open with an article, the sentences begin with a past participle, an article and a conjunction. Variety is the spice of writing; proper pacing provides the spice. Writers sometimes read their stories aloud to hear the pacing. While learning, you may want to count the number of words in each sentence.

Emphasis

Counting the words in sentences and then building in a startling departure from the rhythm is one way to emphasize a point. The short sentence—or the long sentence in a series of short ones—draws attention to itself. But there are other ways to achieve emphasis, the technique of drawing attention to a word, phrase, idea or group of ideas. The devices you can use include story organization, story proportion, sentence ordering, punctuation and repetition.

Traditionally, news stories in newspapers and many internal company publications have been written in the inverted pyramid. That organization emphasizes the lead, the opening paragraph or two. The essence of the message appears at the beginning of the story. In the narrative form, the essence of the message usually appears near the end. The narrative form is common to the news magazines and other publications less concerned with the timeliness of the information. Increasingly, the narrative is being used in newspapers, too. Nearly a month after a jetliner crashed in Washington, D.C. and killed 78 persons, the transcript of the conversation in the cockpit was released. Using the inverted pyramid, United Press International emphasized what it believed to be the important information:

> The cockpit crew of an Air Florida jetliner repeatedly discussed the icing and the weather in their final minutes of conversation before the plane plunged into the Potomac River, tape transcripts showed Thursday.

The New York Times used a modified inverted pyramid to emphasize the significant information and some of the atmosphere:

> The two pilots of a jetliner that crashed in Washington talked repeatedly, often jokingly, about a snowstorm and the buildup of snow on the wings of their own plane and others as they waited to take off. And they differed over the significance of instrument readings even as the plane roared down the runway, only to fall, moments later, into the Potomac River.

By contrast, The Miami Herald elected to subordinate the significant findings by using a modified narrative form:

The doomed pilots of Flight 90 examined their jetliner's wings—and perhaps the wings of other planes—and noticed an ice buildup. They discussed the ice, the blustery weather—at times, casually.

They cursed about it and laughed about it.

However, they took off anyway—only to die instantly minutes later with co-pilot Roger Alan Petit saying: "Larry, we're going down, Larry."

"I know it," Capt. Larry Wheaton said.

The Herald reported the significant information—that ice had built up on the jetliner's wings—but subordinated it to the re-creation of the final seconds. The emphasis was on telling the story, not on telling the news. In an issue dated 10 days later, Time magazine used the narrative form to re-create the scene on the runway:

> As the snow swirled down on Washington that Wednesday afternoon, the drivers creeping past National Airport could barely see their way. Some even parked on the road and stepped out into the blizzard to clean their windshields of the sticky snow before driving farther. On the runways at National, the snow and ice were just as bad. Several of the idling jetliners returned to their bays more than once to be cleared of snow and ice and swabbed with glycol antifreeze.

UPI, the newspapers and Time magazine all emphasized different aspects of the story. The inverted pyramid and narrative forms played important roles in conveying that emphasis.

The space devoted to any aspect of the story—in relation to the length of the story—also determines emphasis. If two-thirds of the story pertains to the weather conditions when the plane crashed, the clear message is that the weather contributed to the crash. But if two-thirds of the story is devoted to reporting verbatim the transcript—even those parts that did not pertain to weather—the story becomes one of the pilots' last minutes rather than what caused the crash. That emphasis of proportion is true of all stories, whether they be spot news or personality profiles.

Within the story, there are four other devices to achieve emphasis: sentence length, which we've already discussed, the order of the sentence, punctuation and repetition.

Normal sentence order is subject-verb. (Or, subject-verb is normal sentence order.) That sequence sometimes results in "loose" sentences, those which, like this one, ramble on long after the main thought has been completed. That's like telling an audience who dunnit and then expecting them to stay around to the end anyway. Periodic sentences, by contrast, do not complete the main thought until the end. This ensures that the reader will see it through. Still, to emphasize you can invert sentences:

> The largest beneficiary of this booming business is none other than the American oil industry.

The American oil industry is the largest beneficiary of this booming business. None other than the American oil industry is the largest beneficiary of this booming business.

The first sentence is periodic: "Who gets it" isn't known until the end. The second sentence is loose. It could end after beneficiary. Inverted, the third sentence emphasizes "who gets it" by abnormal placement. Ideas at the beginning and end of sentences are emphasized naturally. Usually, the end provides more punch than the beginning.

In addition to sentence length and placement within the sentence, there is a third way to provide emphasis. That is to set off an idea—dashes are one way (and parentheses are another)—so that it attracts your reader's attention. Both of these devices should be used sparingly. Marks of emphasis like parentheses and quotation marks around puns should be used about as often as the buzzards return to Hinckley, Ohio.

Repetition

Repetition, however, ought to be seen and heard more often. We have discussed the value of pacing and emphasis. Repetition provides both.

You can repeat both words and forms. Repeating words is one way to provide transitions. It is also a way of emphasizing the word. The Washington Post's Jean White used the technique while reporting on an auction at the fabled J.P. Morgan estate:

It was a time when the very rich were rich together, as F. Scott Fitzgerald has described it; a time of private mansions, private polo fields, private railroad cars, private art collections, private yachts. . . .

By repeating "private," White drives home the idea of wealth.

More often, repetition of form is used. Parallel construction is used both to equate and to contrast. In *Changing of the Guard,* David Broder quotes from a memo by pollster Patrick Caddell:

Americans always believed that their country fought only just wars, and that we did not lose wars like other nations. Then came Vietnam.

Americans always believed that every President would at least try to provide moral leadership—that whatever was wrong with the man, the office itself would right. . . . Then came Nixon and Watergate.

Americans always believed that this country was ruled by the ballot, not the bullet. . . . Then came Dallas and all the horror which has followed. . . .

The repetition of "Americans always believed" followed by the contrast in the shorter sentences is parallel throughout. That parallelism establishes a cadence that is often present when writing is meant to be read aloud. Churchill used the technique often and successfully:

> We shall not flag or fail. We shall go on to the end. We shall fight in France, we shall fight on the seas and oceans, we shall fight with growing confidence and growing strength in the air, we shall defend our island, whatever the cost may be, we shall fight on the beaches, we shall fight on the landing grounds, we shall fight in the fields and in the streets, we shall fight in the hills; we shall never surrender.

The passage could be tightened, but the cadence would be destroyed: "We shall fight in France, on the seas and oceans, with growing confidence and growing strength in the air. . . .

Such a cadence works when it is appropriate to the content. Dick Dougherty, a columnist for the Rochester (N.Y.) Times-Union, wrote a parody of the style:

> Fellow Americans! I am going forward! I am not going backward! I am going forward into the kitchen! And what am I going to do there? Am I going to do the dishes? ("No!" shouted the audience of two, already inflamed by his oratory.)
> Am I going to make a sandwich?
> "No!"
> Am I going to meet the challenge of the Soviet Union with vacillation and confusion?
> "No!" (The crowd of two was going bananas now.)
> No, fellow Americans. I'll tell you what I am going to do.
> I am going to throw away this empty beer can (cheers); I am going to throw this beer can and then, then I am going to go to the refrigerator; I am going to go to the refrigerator and open the door. And (softly now) when I have the door open, when I have the door fully open and light floods the interior (voice level building to full volume now), I am going to reach inside and SEIZE ANOTHER BEER!

Parallelism, which is repetition of form, depends on strict adherence to the pattern. Whether you use parallel nouns or verbs, phrases or clauses, you need to maintain a consistent form. Thus:

> The tornado dropped onto the city Wednesday, killing four persons, injuring seven, and caused $2 million in damage.

should be:

> The tornado dropped onto the city Wednesday, killed four persons, injured seven and caused $2 million in damage.

In the first example, the writer switched from verb to participles and then back to a verb. The rewritten version presents a series of verbs in parallel form.

HANDLING QUOTES
AND ATTRIBUTION

Nothing is more deadly to the rhythm of a story than a quote that doesn't carry its own weight or an attribution that isn't necessary. Too many journalists use quotes extensively. When wisely selected, quotations help tell and personalize a story. When not, they are leaches draining the story of its vitality. And for every quotation, there is the question of attribution, a burden that non-fiction writers must learn to bear more graciously.

Direct quotes enhance journalistic credibility and add the human element in the story. But pick up any newspaper and magazine, and you will see them overused. They are like candy kisses: too many of them are sickening. Fewer direct quotes are not going to damage credibility because with sensory appeal, we have even better ways of writing the human element into the story.

Still if selected carefully, direct quotes are valuable. As a general rule, look for the unexpected, both in form and content.

There is nothing unexpected in this quote from a telecommunications engineer: "Revocation of a franchise usually isn't to the benefit of anybody." A paraphrase would have served as well. When an attorney says, "They didn't hire me because I'm good, even though I am. They hired me because they thought I had an in," that's unexpected content. Unexpected form comes from another attorney: "It's the second coming. Cable is hot, it's an item, it's in."

You can capture emotion in direct quotes—"Lord have mercy on me! I've killed my best friend"—and pathos—"But you know what? I had that gun right up to my head. . . . I couldn't do it. I wanted to, but I didn't have the nerve." Quotes can sum up frustration: "This government is driving me nuts. The forms are so complicated, I have to call my accountant at $35 an hour or my lawyer at $125 just to get a translation." They can sum up vision: "I have no apologies for the federal government being interested in people, in nutrition, education, health and transportation. Who's going to take care of the environment and establish standards: You? Me? Who's going to work out our transportation problems: the B&O Railroad?"

Direct quotes can do all that, but too often they carry only meaningless verbiage. Witness this sample from the front page of a metropolitan paper:

> "No doubt about it," maintained Sen. Dan Quayle, an Indiana Republican who co-sponsored the amendment. "There is bipartisan dissatisfaction with the decision on the MX basing mode. It carries across both sides of the aisle.
> "We've got to bring pressure on the administration," he added, "to come up with a basing mode that is survivable, that is acceptable, and that will be adopted."

To save space and increase understanding, the quotation should have been paraphrased:

Sen. Dan Quayle, the Indiana Republican who co-sponsored the amendment, said legislators in both parties oppose the administration's plan to locate the MX missiles in silos. He said the administration needs to find a way to protect the missiles.

As a general rule:

1. Avoid direct quotes with factual, verifiable information. ("I think we held him to 10 points," the coach said.)
2. Avoid formula writing that calls for direct quote, paraphrase, direct quote, paraphrase. . . .
3. Avoid reporting that consists of getting a couple of quotes.

You don't apply the same criteria to each quote when you are using extended dialogue. You should choose to reproduce a conversation with a person—or run it as a monologue—only when that person is famous, an interesting conversationalist, colorful, has a compelling story to tell or all four. When the subject does not meet at least one of those criteria, your story will be dull at great length.

When Adolf Eichmann, chief of the Gestapo Bureau of Jewish Affairs, was tried for the mass murders of the Jews, Homer Bigart of The New York Times reported on the trial. One of the witnesses was a woman who was buried alive in a grave with hundreds of dead and dying Jews. Building in only an occasional transition, Bigart let her tell the story in her own words:

> "Germans poured into the ghetto and ordered us out of our homes," she said.
> "Suddenly a large truck appeared and Jews were thrown into it. When there was no more room in the truck, others were ordered to run behind it.
> "I ran, carrying my daughter in my arms. There were other mothers running with two, three or four children. Those who stumbled and fell were shot."
> When they had run about three miles, they reached their destination. . . . They had been ordered to disrobe and were standing naked, awaiting execution.
> "I turned my head and saw that about twelve people already had been shot," she said. "My daughter said: 'Mother, why did you make me wear my Sabbath dress? We are being taken to be shot.'
> "And when we were near the grave she cried: 'Why are we waiting? Let us run!'
> "Some of the young people did try to escape, but they were caught immediately and shot on the spot.
> "It was difficult to hold on to the children. They could not understand why we were all pushing nearer the grave, nearer the end of torture for us and the children. . . .'"

To paraphrase a significant portion of that account would be an act of literary insensitivity. Still, even Bigart compressed some of it to maintain the story line. Compression is the process of editing, not of changing what was said or taking the conversation out of context.

A larger problem with extended dialogue is how to handle dialect. Even to consider it, you need both a good ear and a tape recorder. The dialect can be regional, as it was when John McPhee wrote about the New Jersey Pineys, or it can be a combination of regionalism and ethnicity, as it was when Bil Gilbert wrote about Nick Haywood, a black man who had become a one-man, private enterprise, juvenile delinquency prevention program in Kansas City, Mo. McPhee chose not to reproduce the dialect, though he explained several words that are unique to the Pineys' common vocabulary:

> Bill is building a small cranberry bog of his own, "turfing it out" by hand. When he is not working in the bogs, he goes roaming, as he puts it, setting out cross-country on long, looping journeys, hiking about thirty miles in a typical day, in search of what he calls "events"—surprising a buck, or a gray fox, or perhaps a poacher or a man with a still.

Gilbert, on the other hand, used dialect. To reassure readers he wasn't just reinforcing stereotypes, he explained the how and why of what he was doing and concluded, "To render his accent precisely in print is possible, but it may leave the impression that the writer is patronizing Haywood, which is not possible." By explaining his rationale, Gilbert met the problem head-on.

ATTRIBUTION

The special burden the journalist bears is the necessity of attribution. Constant repetition of attribution jars the ear. Some journalists' solution is to eliminate too much of the attribution in the interest of smoother sentences. As we saw in Chapter 2, Teresa Carpenter's Village Voice story on the man who killed Allard Lowenstein was severely criticized for not having enough attribution. Her critics were particularly outraged by this passage:

> After the shooting, in fact, there were rumors that Lowenstein and Sweeney had fallen out as a result of a lover's quarrel. Everyone simply assumed that Lowenstein had approached Sweeney. (Now, from his cell at Rikers Island, Sweeney denies that they ever had a relationship. Once while he and Lowenstein were traveling through Mississippi together, they checked into a motel. According to Sweeny, Lowenstein made a pass and Sweeney rebuffed it. Sweeney is not angry with Lowenstein, he claims. Nor does he feel any shame. It's just that Lowenstein wasn't always above board.)

Carpenter never interviewed Sweeney. The information apparently came through Sweeney's attorney and another unnamed source. But the passage does not reflect this.

Journalists walk a delicate tightrope between the need to establish the source of information and the effort to make the story readable. At stake is our credibility.

There are, however, at least five ways to deal with the problem:

1. You do not need attribution more than once in a paragraph for the same speaker if no other name appears in that paragraph or if it is clear who is speaking. Too many writers use attribution in the first sentence of the paragraph and repeat it at the end.
2. You do not need attribution with every direct quote when you have only one speaker. The context will show whether the attribution is needed. If it is clear who the speaker is in the paragraph preceeding the direct quote, you do not have to hook another attribution to the quote.
3. You do not have to attribute factual, verifiable material. Information such as "The building was seven stories high," should not be in quotes and does not have to be attributed unless the reporter is unsure of its veracity.
4. You do not have to write, "He says he did . . ." when there is no reason to believe it's not true. Simply write, "He did. . . ."
5. You can use a comprehensive attribution when you are introducing a version of events from a single source. For instance: "According to police reports, this was the sequence of events leading to the fight:" What follows may be a paragraph or several paragraphs. The attribution does not have to be repeated throughout them.

Most of these guidelines are put into practice in the following excerpt. The lined words represent excess attribution. Read it once with the attribution and once without.

> "For us jobless and homeless, here is almost like heaven," says Clement Carls, a temporary resident at Everyday People in Springfield.
> An alcoholic who has no job or money, he is determined to quit drinking. He came to Springfield for counseling and became a resident of Everyday People.
> The agency is a government-funded, volunteer organization set up to help homeless and helpless alcoholics who want to quit drinking.
> Carls, 40, is from Chicago. He used to be a worker in a steel cable factory there. At 17, he started to drink.
> "At the beginning, I just felt good, got high," Carl says. "But later, I was addicted and drank all day until I blacked out."
> When he was drunk, ~~he says~~ he felt lost. He missed work. Then, ~~he says,~~ he lost his job, his car, and finally, his wife.
> ~~He says~~ he quit drinking in 1970 and stayed away from alcohol for six years. "I started drinking again last year because I had too much time on my hands," Carls says.
> He drank at home, in the bar and on the street. Sometimes he started fights. He quit a second time.
> "I have caused my mother too much worry," ~~Carls says.~~ "I felt guilty. This time I'm quitting for good," ~~he says.~~

Attribution should bear the burden of proving its necessity. Ask "why" when you use it. If there is a chance the reader will be confused, use it. If not, don't.

All of these creative writing techniques, from the inventive use of imagery to the unobtrusive use of attribution, are but tools. The writer, like the craftsman, knows the limits and the potential of those tools.

5

structuring
the story

The collapsed skywalk had stilled the big band music just four days earlier when two editors approached David Hacker in the Kansas City Times newsroom. Mike Davies and Chris Waddle wanted a retrospective on the Hyatt Regency tragedy, in which 111 people lost their lives. They asked Hacker to do it in human terms and to do it under deadline pressure.

In the next 36 hours, Hacker persuaded four widows to talk to him, debated the story's ethical aspects and completed the reporting. At 7 a.m. of the sixth day after the tragedy, he sat down to write the story of the last day of each of the four couples. Eight hours and 7,000 words later, Hacker finished. He gave it to his editors, went to dinner, returned home and cried.

He cried, not about his own ordeal, but for the victims and survivors. The story, he said later, "was remarkably easy to do, with the structure I had built."

Using the time and temperature as guideposts, Hacker told the story of "The Day the Music Stopped" chronologically. This is how he began:

> When Nancy Jonas poked her husband, Bob, in the back to wake him up the morning of Friday, July 17, her elbow touched skin. It was hot, and Bob was wearing as little as possible, which was next to nothing. In fact, the only thing he had on was his beard, under which was tucked a double chin. . . .

She thought the beard fit him nicely as she rolled back over at 6:30, after the radio alarm had gone off, turning on gentle music. The radio was on her side of the bed. So she was his alarm clock. "I hate the raucous noise of an alarm," she said. . . .

Exactly 44 blocks away (but you've got to skitter around the Meadowbrook Golf and Country Club, and the blocks in the 87th and Roe area get to be pretty big) at 8021 Pennsylvania, on the Missouri side of the state line, Louis and Mary Katherine Bottenberg were still asleep when Bob Jonas was puttering around the bathroom. It would be an hour and a half yet before they got up. Bob and Mary Kay were retired, and time and what they did were their own inventions. The day began with music, and often ended that way, for Lou was a musician of uncommon originality and enthusiasm. He played the dulcimer, mandolin, guitar and even the player piano. When he wasn't fiddlin' or twiddlin', he was dancing. In the Waldo area, where he and Mary Kay lived, his clog dancing had made him something of a celebrity. . . .

But at 6024 Morningside Drive, in the Brookside section of Kansas City, 27 blocks north of the Bottenbergs, Friday was stirring at 6:45 a.m. at the elegant home of Jerold and Jacqueline Rau. Theirs is a 14-room Georgian mansion, restored by the childless couple. Inside, Adams-style furnishings (protected by an elaborate anti-burglar system) make every room look like a Plaza show window. The first to rise was the Baroness Myriah Souflette du Grandville, a 7-year-old toy French poodle. She had risen from her wicker-basket bed, bought at Azizy le Rideau, a French village. Sharply, at a quarter of seven each morning, she'd ballet her way over to Jerold's side of the bed, stand up and scratch the covers. This, Jackie said, was Myriah's way of telling him that it was time for her tummy to be rubbed. . . .

Next door at 6034 Morningside Drive, where Angela and James Paolozzi lived, things tended to be more chaotic. Jim was 39, Angie 34, and then the fun began: Jimmy was 16; Tina, 13; Michael, 5; and the twins, Melissa and Jessica, were 20 months old.

This morning, though, Angie said: "We got up a little later than usual. Jim wasn't feeling so good. We thought about canceling out the plans for the tea dance that evening."

Friday, July 17.
Seven o'clock in the morning. The temperature was 79. Twelve hours left. . . .
For the men—Bob, Louis, Jerold and Jim—a half-day of living left.
For the women—Nancy, Mary Kay, Jackie and Angie—a sisterhood of those who learn that death may destroy bad marriages, but it only splinters good ones and to survive you just have to pick out the slivers.

Eight o'clock. The temperature was still 79 degrees. Eleven hours left.

For Hacker, purpose determined structure. To permit readers to share the grief and perhaps to participate in the healing process, Hacker recreated the last day in detail. The time and temperature permitted him to tie together the lives of four couples who otherwise had only death in common.

What all non-fiction writers have in common is a necessity to choose an appropriate structure to tell their stories. Chronology is the oldest story form. As Hacker and others demonstrate daily, it is still useful. But there are other forms, and in this chapter, we will explain what they are and how you can use them.

They are the inverted pyramid, the focus structure, the essay and the suspended interest structure.

INVERTED PYRAMID

The inverted pyramid and the Model T were contemporaries. Now we are driving K-cars, but the inverted pyramid remains the basic story structure of newspaper and electronic journalists. It is the most efficient structure yet devised for communicating news quickly and clearly. In simplest terms, the information is broken into five categories: who, what, where, when and how. Often, these days, journalists are adding "why." The writer ranks each of the categories in descending order of importance and then begins with the most important:

> WASHINGTON (AP)—A proposed constitutional amendment favoring a balanced budget squeaked through the Senate with just two votes to spare Wednesday and headed for an uncertain fate in the House.

In this one sentence, the writer answers who (the amendment), what (passed), where (the Senate), when (Wednesday) and how (by two votes.)

To newspaper and broadcast journalists, this form is so common that few give it a second thought. Some print journalists even think it is an anachronism. Yet, it still has an important function to fulfill. It conveys information quickly and efficiently, and because it can be trimmed quickly from the bottom, it facilitates newspaper make-up. Its use, in modified form, could even be extended into corporations where managers who get lengthy reports often have to skip to the last page to read the recommendation or conclusion. The same report written with the most important information first—the recommendations—would save that manager time. Its principles are also applicable to newsletters and memos. The ability to recognize the most important elements of a story—and rank them—is essential to all writers.

To successfully use the inverted pyramid, you must be able to define its basic elements. For instance, you may define "what" as the meeting rather than what happened at the meeting. Move from the general to the specific. General:

> The City Council met last night at Municipal Center.

Specific:

> The City Council last night fired the city manager and named a search committee to look for a new one.

Saving the reader time is what the inverted pyramid does best, but in the hands of the creative, it can also be entertaining. Stan Benjamin wrote this lead for Newhouse News Service on a story about how Saudi Arabia dominates OPEC:

> It is written in the desert sands: Twelve horses harnessed with an elephant will go where the elephant wants to go.
> So may it be with the 13 tribes of OPEC.

Benjamin used a time-delay device in his inverted pyramid. The first two paragraphs tell, but not explicitly. It is a space-efficient way to hook readers. The explicit lead plays off the hook:

> Sheik Almed Zaki Yamani, petroleum minister of Saudi Arabia, is counting on it, and so are the world's oil consumers as they watch Yamani try to reduce and unify the divergent voices of the Organization of Petroleum Exporting Countries.

Another journalist was writing a story about a doctor who lost his job at a Catholic teaching hospital when it was disclosed he had attempted to inseminate a lesbian artificially. The story began this way:

> "All we wanted was a baby," the lesbian said.

The hook is set firmly. The news—that the lesbian cost the doctor a job—followed immediately.

The opening paragraph, or lead, in any story structure is important, but writers of the inverted pyramid must learn to be especially brief and interesting. Writers of other story forms usually have more time, even if only a few more paragraphs, in which to set the hook.

While the inverted pyramid is relatively easy to manage for most stories, it, too, can take several twists when the writer is dealing with many important elements. Investigative or enterprise reporters often find themselves with reams of material of equal or near-equal value. Yet, because investigative reporters are revealing information, the inverted pyramid is often the logical story structure.

The priority of information in investigative stories varies from story to story, but the essential information usually can be reduced to "Who's doing (or failing to do) what to whom." That is often followed by a summary of the findings that foreshadow what the rest of the article is about. Foreshadowing—or teasing the reader—is an essential element of all story structures. High in the story, the reader should learn how you or your publication discovered this information and why anyone should care. That element often is referred to as the "so what" of stories, as in "Okay, you've spent three months investigating and have 20 notebooks full of information. So what?" The "so what" is the significance of the findings.

For investigative reporters, then, the essential elements of the inverted pyramid consist not just simply of who, what, where, when and how but also:

Who's doing (or failing to do) what to whom.
Summary of findings and foreshadowing.
How the investigation was conducted.
The "so what" factor.

(Details on how to execute this structure can be found in Chapter 6.)

While this approach communicates the essential information clearly, quickly and concisely, it does have one shortcoming: It lacks a vehicle for building the human element into the opening. The focus structure solves that problem.

FOCUS STRUCTURE

This is the news The Wall Street Journal reported on Dec. 7, 1981:

> In November, with the overall jobless rate at 8.4%, white-collar unemployment hit its highest level—4.2%, or 2.7 million persons—since the record of 5.3% set during the 1973–75 recession.

Recognizing that percentages and seven-digit numbers do not drama make, the Journal writer delayed that information until the sixth paragraph. What readers were treated to first was a protagonist:

> Last year, Alan Cremer was invited by his boss at W.R. Grace & Co. to tag along with him to a new, $40,000-a-year job at Data Terminal Systems Inc. in Maynard, Mass. Mr. Cremer jumped at the chance to become the latter company's director of manpower training and development.
>
> Today, Mr. Cremer is out of a job, having been fired by the very man who had urged him to leave Grace. The word to let him go had come from the top brass at Data Terminal, who, in order to cut costs, were firing 70 white-collar employees . . .

"Don't write about Man," E.B. White advised. "Write about a man." He could have as well said, "Don't write about 2.7 million unemployed white-collar workers; write about one of them." The structure permits the writer to focus on an interesting story, usually of one person, before turning to the universal theme. The structure permits journalists to perform two important functions: Make the story interesting and put it in context. No periodical is taking advantage of the literary techniques available to it if it ignores the power of people to attract people. And no periodical is fulfilling its function if it tells stories about the Alan Cremers of the world without relating them to others being effected the same way.

Out of these needs was born a structure that permits writers both to add humanity to a story and process information. The structure works like this:

1. Open with a person, anecdote or situation that illustrates the theme of the story.
2. Provide a transition to the theme paragraph.

3. Explain the story line in the theme paragraph.
4. Tease the reader.
5. Provide details to support the theme.
6. Close, preferably by referring to someone or something introduced in the opening.

Let's look at each of these parts of the focus structure.

Opening with a person—an Alan Cremer—to illustrate the theme of the story is the most common opening in the focus structure, but writers can also open either with anecdotal or situation leads. For all of them, one test is whether they are pertinent to the story: Do they illustrate the theme in an interesting way?

Let's look at examples of anecdotal and situation leads. A reporter for The Miami Herald reported testimony verbatim to build an anecdotal lead:

> LAKE BUENA VISTA, Fla.—It happened in broad daylight on Main Street U.S.A.
>
> "I was watching the parade, and this Disney character came towards me," Pennsylvania housewife Patricia Reinsel recalled under oath. "He walked right toward me . . . he was just kind of dancing around . . . and I was kicked."
>
> Attorney: "Describe the character as best you can."
>
> Reinsel: "It was a big brown dog with long whiskers and long ears."
>
> Attorney: "Do you think it was Pluto?"
>
> Reinsel: "Yes . . . yes!!"
>
> Hi ho, hi ho, it's off to court we go.
>
> Welcome to Walt Disney World, home of Tomorrowland, Frontierland—and sometimes Litigationland, where tourists of all shapes and sizes sue the ears off Mickey Mouse.
>
> "We're a target defendant," acknowledges lawyer John H. Ward, who defends many of Disney's negligence cases. . . .

The lead is a story within a story. It gives way to the theme paragraph, which informs us that Disney World is sued often.

Recreating a situation that illustrates the theme of the story is another effective way to weave an interesting opening. It requires reporting in detail. When done well, the opening sounds like a scene from a novel. This one, however, is from a newspaper:

> Thick, damp strands of white hair stick to his forehead or tumble over his glasses as he leans against his new blue sedan. Amid the steady hum of Saturday night traffic, he protests to the officer that the light was not working, but the words stick in a too-dry mouth. As the red warning light of the intersection flashes over them at two-second intervals, Columbia police officer Joe Fagiolo gently urges the man, a 56-year-old college teacher, to walk an imagined line on the unpaved shoulder of West Boulevard.
>
> "Heel to toe, sir. Put your arms out at your sides for balance," Fagiolo says.
>
> The teacher stiffly raises his arms, but it is too late. With the first tight, lurching step, he is down.
>
> "Have you had anything intoxicating to drink tonight?" Fagiolo asks.

"No, for God's sake," the man says. "Only three."
Fagiolo arrests him on suspicion of driving while intoxicated.

That opening sets up the transition to the theme paragraph:

> More than 350 people have been arrested on charges of DWI in Boone County so far this year, more than for any other offense.
>
> "It's a big problem here," says Assistant Prosecuting Attorney Skip Walther.
>
> Despite the seriousness of the problem and the fact that drinking drivers caused at least 17,300 accidents in Missouri last year—including half of all accidents involving death or injury—a study by the Columbia Missourian shows that:
>
> —Only one-third of those arrested on suspicion of DWI are actually charged with that offense by the Boone County prosecuting attorney's office.
>
> —The other two-thirds are allowed to plead guilty to a lesser offense, a practice that lightens sentences and allows them to drive.
>
> —The prosecuting attorney's office has followed a policy of consistently reducing DWI charges for first offenders even when tests show the driver's blood alcohol content to be well above the legal minimum for intoxication. . . .

Fiction writers create situations; non-fiction writers recreate them. Done well, these vignettes invite readers to participate in a real-life experience.

Situational leads often take more space to set up than most newspaper reporters can afford, although even in newspapers, this structure is found with increasing frequency. Some publications allow you more freedom and space to craft an introduction. When Ron Rosenbaum wrote about the lure of questionable cancer cures, he used the basic focus structure but set up the opening slowly. His prize-winning story in New West magazine began this way:

> The Captain rapped on the door of my hotel room promptly at 6 a.m. He was eager to get this expedition under way. He had a decision to make, and his time was running out.
>
> First of all, just 30 hours remained on his VA hospital pass. If he didn't make it back in time, they might find out about his peculiar below-the-border mission. Worse, they might search his room and confiscate whatever magic potion he managed to bring back.
>
> And the time was fast approaching when they were scheduled to do that CAT-scan on the Captain's liver, get a picture, give a local habitation and a name to that vexing shadow on his last X ray. They had already cut a malignancy out of his intestines—this shadow could be the dread metastasis.
>
> "No use pretending you're brave or whistling past the graveyard," the Captain told me as we headed south on 405. "I know I've got it again."
>
> But this time the Captain was going to be ready with a plan of his own. That's why he'd asked to hitch a ride with me on my exploratory trip to the cancer clinics of Tijuana. There were at least a half dozen establishments down there offering every kind of exotic therapy and esoteric substance driven below the border by U.S. authorities—everything from the mysterious decades-old Hoxsey elixir to coffee enema cures, fetal sheep cell injections and three varieties of metabolic enzyme treatments. The Captain wanted to scout them all so he'd have his escape route ready when the CAT-scan delivered its diagnosis.

"I know surgery is not the answer," the Captain declared. "I can say that from experience. I took chemotherapy and it was rough. I couldn't take it anymore, and from experience, from the statistics, I know it doesn't work. So they told me, 'Why don't you try immunotherapy?' That was equally rough. They inject dead cells in an alcohol base into your back. I still have the scars. Devilish rough. You can see it in the doctors' eyes—they know they're up against something they can't beat."

The Captain does not say the word "rough" from the perspective of a man who's lived a life of ease. Not counting his wartime Marine Corps service, he's spent most of his 60 years working as a mining geologist in one rough place or another, prospecting for platinum in the Bering Strait, seeking rare earths and precious metals in the feverish interiors of Central America. The Captain never minded the physical privations of the prospector's life, he told me—it was malignant fate that had treated him roughly.

"Had a reef of platinum off the Aleutians," he sighed. "Would have made my fortune. I was back in the States getting ready to sell shares of it when a goddamn earthquake wiped it out."

The same thing happened down in Yucatan, the Captain said. Titanium this time, a sizzling vein of it. Another earthquake and it was gone.

These reverses left the Captain—who has no fortune or family to fall back on—at the mercy of the VA when the malignancy first showed up. He complains bitterly of the degrading, no privacy, prisonlike confinement at the hospital, but he has nowhere else to go.

Still, circumstances have not deprived the Captain of his drive, his prospector's instinct, and this time he is on the trail of something more valuable than any of the precious metals he sought in the past. This time the Captain is prospecting for a cancer cure.

The presence of the Captain immediately signals that this is not a technical piece on underground cancer cures but a story about why people who would otherwise know better succumb to their lure. The ten thousand people a year who travel to Tijuana's cancer clinics are merely a statistic; Captain is Rosenbaum's Ahab, a non-fiction protagonist. In the fifth paragraph, we learn about the scope of the clinics; in the eleventh, we find the story line: "This time the Captain is prospecting for a cancer cure." The line is followed quickly by the transition into the body of the story: "So are we all, of course."

The transition

The transition between the opening example and the theme paragraph is essential to the success of the structure. Without it, many readers will fail to make the connection between the example and the story theme. At its simplest, the transition says, "This person (or anecdote or situation) is representative of many." In Mitchell C. Lynch's Wall Street Journal story about the unemployed white-collar workers, his transition starts to put Alan Cremer in context:

> As the recession worsens, conditions that have blue-collar workers standing in unemployment lines are beginning to take their toll of white-collar workers, a category that includes executives, professionals, managers, clerks and other largely salaried employes not primarily involved in manual labor.

If Alan Cremer doesn't fit that definition, then he is not pertinent to the story and should not be used as the focus. Pertinence is the test of whether the lead is appropriate. When the focus structure was being developed by magazine writers in the 1920s, leads often had so little relationship to the story theme that it took either great tolerance or no critical faculties to continue reading the stories. The genre has been refined throughout the years, however, so that today writers for both newspapers and magazines use it to perform its dual functions—informing and entertaining—successfully.

Theme paragraph

In the inverted pyramid, the most important information is presented in the first paragraph. In the focus structure, it is presented in the theme paragraph or paragraphs, which appear near, but not at the top. Remember that in the story about Cremer, the theme—in that case, the news—appeared in the sixth paragraph. The theme in Rosenbaum's story about underground cancer cures maintains his informal, first-person tone:

> But this time the Captain was going to be ready with a plan of his own. That's why he'd asked to hitch a ride with me on my exploratory trip to the cancer clinics in Tijuana. . . .

That theme paragraph gives way to the narrative. Rosenbaum develops the story chronologically. By contrast, Lynch presents the evidence to support his story line that white-collar workers are feeling the pinch in descending order of importance.

As you may have noticed by now, this chapter is written using the focus structure. We opened with an example of a writer—David Hacker—who had to select a structure appropriate to his content. That done, we moved to the chapter's theme statement:

> Chronology is the oldest story form. As Hacker and others demonstrate daily, it is still useful. But there are others, and in this chapter, we will explain what they are and how you can use them. . . .

You'll hear more of Hacker later.

Foreshadowing

At the carnival sideshows, you may see the fat man or the dancing girls for free. That's the tease. The promise is that there is more inside.

When writers tease, it's called foreshadowing. Those writers who are good at it are like the carnival barker: They can whip the tent flap open just far enough and long enough to whet your appetite.

Rosenbaum teased: "This time the Captain is prospecting for a cancer cure." Will he find it? Rosenbaum placed this tease at the end of his introduction.

In newspapers and some magazines, where leads to stories written in structures other than the inverted pyramid may consist of three to six paragraphs, the tease can appear anywhere near the top of the story. Usually, though, it is either in the theme paragraph or soon after it. In many magazines, where introductions replace leads, the tease usually come before the body or narrative of the story. When the Philadelphia Inquirer recreated the disaster at the Three Mile Island nuclear power plant, the magazine-like story was nearly nine newspaper pages long. The introduction, fifteen paragraphs long, is a masterfully written tease. It reaches its climax in these two lines:

> The story from outside was hair-raising enough to a nation confronted by the unknown.
> The story from the inside is more alarming yet.

For only a second, the tent flap is swished open. *"The story from inside is more alarming yet."* And if you will come into the tent, reader, you too will learn the inside story.

Non-fiction writers often neglect to foreshadow the story; good fiction writers lead readers on as if they were dropping chocolates down a trail. The taste is irresistible.

The good writing in Noriko Sawada's Ms. Magazine memoir of her life as a youngster is also irresistible:

> Had I been able to forgive my mother during her lifetime and tell her so, I might have spared myself years of feeling hagaii ("itchy teeth," Japanese for helpless anguish tinged with frustration). I had long buried the events that shaped me into a mother-hating adult until they surfaced one evening during a sex seminar when I was well into middle age. Its leaders, in order to purge me of the naughtiness I attribute to sex and the guilt I assume for participating in it, exposed—no, overexposed—me via film to nudity. I had already watched male and female frontal nudes superimposed one upon the other, dissolve and coalesce into unisexual blobs, until I felt no shock, no shame, only boredom at the sight of another naked body.
>
> Then, as I viewed vagina after vagina, topped with full or sparse curly hair and bracketed by limp vulvas—overkill again—my mind raced back to my adolescence and an altercation with my mother when she had so enraged me with her deceit that I vowed never to trust her again. For my story to make sense, however, I first must tell about my mother's early life that had the impact of a fist upon mine.

Sawada brings us to the climax—to an altercation she had as an adolescent with her mother—then unexpectantly backs off, closes the tent. First, she says, I must tell you about my mother's early life. The hook is firmly set.

The technique of foreshadowing is not confined to introductions; you can use it as often as it occurs naturally in the narrative. For instance, longer stories that have natural breaks often benefit from teases at the end of each section. Foreshadowing permits you to move into the body of the story with a promise that something interesting will unfold. It it doesn't, the writer is no better than the illusionist. Writing can't be done with mirrors. Techniques such as foreshadowing help bait the reader, but good writers don't promise more than they can deliver. Unlike the carny, who sometimes has disappeared by the time the show lets out, the writer must stick around for the conclusion.

The body

Perhaps it seems like it took a long time to get here to the body of the story, the primary reason we are reporting and writing. We've introduced our protagonist, we've crafted the transition and stated the theme. We've even been a bit of a tease. Now, at last, we are here. But it really hasn't been all that long: usually as little as three and as many as eight or ten paragraphs.

How the body of the story unfolds depends on the purpose of the story. Is the story revealing the results of an investigation? The information usually will be presented in descending order of importance. Is the story a recreation of an event? It usually will be told in chronological order. Is the story primarily nonfiction entertainment? The writer may collapse time, change sequence or use chronology. Whatever the form, the writer often finds it necessary to take a sideroad occasionally. Flashbacks are one way. Sawada used the technique to move the reader back to her mother's childhood. The trick is to craft an effective transition. Signal your turns for your readers.

Entertain them too. Anecdotes are oases in the body of any story. Even when you are enjoying a long trip, you need a rest. An anecdote provides a smile or at least diversion. In Saul Pett's magnificent retrospective about Franklin Roosevelt for the Associated Press, he built this oasis into the middle of his text:

> Through a thousand competing pressures and details, he appeared imperturbably on top of life. With equal aplomb, he took epic calls from Winston Churchill and one from a son asking if the President knew of a diaper service in Washington.

If anecdotes aren't worth their weight in gold, they are at least worth something, as one enterprising American found out. He wrote Kipling, "I understand you are selling literature for $1 a word. I enclose $1. Please send me a sample."

Kipling kept the dollar and replied, "Thanks."

The American wrote back that he had sold the anecdote for $2. He enclosed 45 cents worth of stamps—half the profits minus postage.

The close

The inverted pyramid is like most lizards: cutting off their tails doesn't affect them. Often the victim of too little space, the inverted pyramid is designed to be cut from the bottom. Little premium is placed on the ending. But writers can't be so blasé about the ending of other story structures. The close, the denouement for fiction writers, gives the writer an opportunity to come full circle. When you have opened with a person who illustrates the theme of the story, the close gives you an opportunity to turn your attention to that person again. In carefully crafted closings the writer ties up loose ends as Pett did, when he wrote about Franklin Roosevelt. His story began with two people:

> It hit people in different ways, all of them bad.
> The first thing that happened in Paul Bethke's house, near Loveland, Colo., was that a dream began to die. He had yearned to be a school teacher but now, at 20, he had to drop out of Colorado State Teacher's College.
> His parents, who ran a small farm, were stone broke. He had one pair of pants, corduroys, and he washed them every week. He drifted, desperate for a job. He would ride boxcars, a hobo, just one step ahead of the railroad cops, this man who wanted to be a teacher.
> The first thing that happened in Harold Ions' house, on a day in 1932 in Ferndale, Mich., was that his father was laid off after nearly 30 years at Ford.
> Then, when they couldn't pay the bills, they lost their electricity. Then, when they couldn't meet the monthly mortgage payment of $35, the bank foreclosed and they lost their home.

Pett then tells how FDR pulled America out of the Depression. Along the way, we are offered glimpses of how Bethke and Ions started rebuilding their lives as beneficiaries of New Deal programs. Pett closed with them, too:

> There is still no official monument to Franklin Roosevelt in Washington, D.C., but out in Colorado and Michigan and across the land, monuments exist in the lives of ordinary people.
> Paul Bethke fulfilled his dream of being a teacher. He taught government and political science for 22 years, doubled as football coach, and ended up as superintendent of schools. He has voted mostly Democratic through the years.
> Harold Ions, the auto worker, has voted only Democratic for 48 years. He now has three children, 11 grandchildren and three great-grandchildren.
> In the family as a whole, there are eight homes, 15 cars and 16 television sets. . . .
> And in the twist of circumstances, when one generation takes for granted what another didn't have, when one man's progress becomes another man's concern over high taxes and the excesses of the welfare state, Harold Ion's son, Mickey, also an auto worker, voted for Ronald Reagan.

The denouement. We have a few loose ends of our own to wrap up. First, let's look in on Alan Cremer:

> Mr. Cremer, who has a Ph.D in behavioral studies, has had to vacate his apartment and move in with relatives. Nine days before he was fired, he had bought a new car that he now expects to have trouble paying installments on.
> His job hunt, which began in September, has been discouraging. "They tell me that maybe things will change next month," he says. "I can wait another month."

The protagonist ends it in his own words. Strong quotations make excellent endings.

Now back to Noriko Sawada:

After her funeral, after all the company had gone, my father handed me the missing pieces of the puzzle. He told me about my mother's early life and the baby that she had borne, and about the pact of silence she had sworn him to. I protested that he should have told me sooner; after all, I was no longer a child. But of course he couldn't. Only my mother's death released him from his promise. . . .

I wept for a woman who gamely wore her hair shirt of guilt and who was so perverted by the experience that she could not alter the fatal course of her relationship with her own daughter. I wept for a mother who became grotesque in her daughter's eyes, an object for pity.

I wept for myself.

And finally, let's return to Rosenbaum:

I don't know what's in that Hoxsey tonic, don't want to know, in fact, but having immersed myself in the mystique and made a pilgrimage to the shrine, I have a strange feeling—yes, a false hope, the American Cancer Society would call it—that the old-fashioned elixir might do me some good someday. I hope it helped the Captain.

ESSAYS

The Montaignes and the Bacons, the Swifts and the Lambs live on today in the periodical press. Their work is not labeled essays; these days that term seems reserved for English composition class assignments. Today's essays emerge as editorials, as columns, as stories. What they have in common is structure: opening statement, body and close. What they have in common in content is the presence of the writer.

The broadness of that definition indicates the scope and flexibility of the essay. Editorial writers and commentators use the structure to advocate; columnists use it to advocate, inform, entertain, or all three; reporters use it to tell stories. As writers become more adept, they weave anecdotes, description and analogies through the text as appropriate. Purpose determines appropriateness. A somber discussion of whether the United States ought to sell wheat to Russia probably would not be enhanced by a joke about a Kansas farmer. It might be served though, to recreate scenes of Kansas wheat fields or the bulging grain elevators throughout the Midwest.

Norris Alfred, the owner of the weekly Polk (Neb.) Progress, responded with homespun humor when he was asked how he writes editorials. As a narrative device, he introduced his readers to a great-grandmother who is one of his correspondents. He called her the Progress Swedish Philosopher because she is a fountain of sayings that are simple but wise. Rather than saying that you must write editorials often to write well, Alfred tells this story:

I have been writing editorials for more than 20 years, which I consider staying within the guidelines as stated by the Progress Swedish Philosopher. She is convinced we are on this earth to do something. While lecturing the other folders—the editor; Barb the linotype operator; and Barb's two sons, 6-year-old Stevie, the apprentice printer, and 1-year-old Timmy, the assistant apprentice—on the evils of sloth, she declared, "If you don't do anything you get out of practice."

I'm keeping in practice. I have discovered the only way to learn to write is to write and write and write. . . .

That's a far cry from the formality of Bacon and Johnson. Hugh Sidey's warm and confident tones in his weekly essays in Time magazine contrast with the style, cadence and tone of James Kilpatrick's syndicated newspaper columns, but both are master craftsmen. Here's Sidey sharing with us an intimate look at a White House meeting as he opens an essay:

Months ago, in the first meeting on tax increases, Ronald Reagan sat at the Cabinet table and indifferently thumbed the folder that had been placed before him. He had the air of a man unconvinced, unenthusiastic and disengaged. He read the notes in front of him as if they were an unfamiliar script.

One of the participants in that meeting concluded as he watched the President that Reagan really carried a fundamental distrust of the figures being showered on him, showing huge deficits to come and continuing high interest rates. "What's wrong with Wall Street?" Reagan grumped more than once. . . .

Sidey concludes his essay by drawing a general conclusion from the specific instance of Reagan's turnabout on a tax increase:

But if Reagan has grown bigger than supply-side economics, if he has grasped the meaning of presidential leadership and felt the exhilaration of achieving rather than preaching, he is more likely to succeed in the challenges ahead.

There is another hope held tenderly by some of Reagan's supporters and even a few of his adversaries. It is that he has also escaped his obsession with being consistent. Reagan believes inconsistency discredited Jimmy Carter. That bit of history has some truth, but, as always, one bit is an imperfect guide for other times. Carter was perceived to change positions not for the nation's good but for his personal political fortunes. If Ronald Reagan understood what he said last week about acting for all Americans, it could be the most important declaration of his presidency. That is true consistency.

Sidey writes in soothing tones. His choice of words ("hope held tenderly") and his sentence cadence, is relaxed. Kilpatrick's sentences strut through his essays:

The proposed constitutional amendment to compel a balanced federal budget offers a regrettable but familiar combination often seen on Capitol Hill. The resolution is a mishmash of good intentions and bad law. . . .

The resolution adopted by the Senate on Aug. 4 is flawed in a dozen ways. It undertakes to write statutory law into the Constitution, and this always is a bad business. In Section 2 of the amendment, it is proposed to limit the rate of increase in annual receipts, but the formula by which this would be fixed is a formula composed of algebra and moonbeams. . . .

If we want balanced budgets, the answer lies not in the straw fetters of this amendment, but in the election of responsible representatives. The whole House and a third of the Senate will be up for election in November. If the deficits get worse, let us blame them—but let us blame ourselves too.

Kilpatrick's presence is unmistakable. So is Sidey's. That's not surprising, given their position as columnists. But the same presence is also available in all essays. In stories, that presence ranges from the obvious "I," to the subtle choice of scenes, even words. Advocacy essays leap from the pages of magazines as diverse as Harper's and Mother Jones. Reporters are present in the essays in Sports Illustrated, Esquire, Atlantic and Washington Monthly. A writer's presence is detectable through the writer's attitude. Rosenbaum, for instance, was not advocating, but we clearly knew his attitude toward underground cancer cures. We recognize, too, that John Pekkanen, writing in The Washingtonian, admires Dr. Paul Adkins, then chairman of surgery at the George Washington University Medical School:

In his neighborhood on Kirkwood Drive in Bethesda—a tree-lined street of large, comfortable homes—he was the resident poet, always called upon to write funny poems or limericks for birthdays and anniversaries.

At the hospital he wore quite another face. There he was first and foremost a surgeon: decisive, hard-headed, willing to take greater risks than most. He was a man certain of himself and at the same time shy to an extreme.

The surgical residents he loved to teach called him "The Boss." Virtually all of the younger residents were in the words of a GW colleague, "scared as hell of him." He seldom abided small talk. His sarcasm could be biting and his glare intimidating. But those residents who progressed steadily in the residency program began to realize there was more to him than the stern face. By their third or fourth year they came to understand that at least part of their fear was misplaced. They understood that he jealously guarded his privacy and revealed little of his sensitivity or sense of humor to those he didn't know well. They came to realize that it was because he was lost in thought that he often walked down the corridors of the hospital oblivious to the people who said hello to him.

Only one attribution here. The rest is Pekkanen's evaluation. Pekkanen spent weeks with Dr. Adkins and others at the university's hospital, and although this is a story about Adkins, the writer is present without ever using "I." This is saturation reporting; the story ran 30 magazine pages. It, too, is an essay.

Essay, then, is a broad term. How it is executed depends on the writer's purpose. If it is explanatory, as some editorials and columns are, the writer marshals facts. If it is argumentative, the writer draws general conclusions from specific instances (inductive reasoning) or applies a general truth to a specific instance (deductive reasoning). If it is descriptive, the writer recreates scenes, events, encounters, in the same way that a writer would set up a situational lead for a story. All the variations of essays have this in common, though: They require a clear theme statement, evidence to support it and a conclusion. When Time's Lance Morrow wrote about the war West Texas ranchers wage on mesquite, his theme sentence appeared in the fourth paragraph, after readers had already learned what mesquite is: "The rancher enjoys with his mesquite roughly the relationship that Wile E. Coyote maintains with the Road Runner in the children's cartoon; the rancher will try anything short of nuclear weapons to conquer mesquite. He even talks about it in vaguely military terms." Following that general statement are examples of how ranchers try to destroy the mesquite:

> Some stretches of Tom Green County look like the Argonne Forest after a month of shelling; dead black mesquite trees, torn out of the ground, lie in a vast twisted litter. Vultures like to sit in sinister profile upon the dead trees; they give the scene an eerie stylized hellishness. This particular mesquite has been the victim of chaining and spraying: crop-dusting planes swoop in low over the range and spray a chemical called TORDON 225E onto the mesquite. A year or more later, a pair of bulldozers about a hundred yards apart make their way across the same area dragging an enormous ship's anchor chain between them.

While the theme statement appears to be an overstatement, the examples lend it plausibility. Points should be discussed, not merely stated.

If that is done, when the reader reads the conclusion it will be apparent, at least, how the writer arrived there. That's true whether you are frantically urging the City Council to action or musing over the renewal of spring. The theme has been stated, the evidence has been presented, and the conclusion is rendered. That done, stop.

SUSPENDED INTEREST

The most radical departure from the story structures we have discussed is also the simplest. The suspended interest form is merely another name for a pure chronology; you heed the king's advice in "Alice in Wonderland." Asked where to start, he replied, "Begin at the beginning and go on till you come to the end; then stop." Few non-fiction chronological accounts start at the beginning and run until the end. Most start with an exciting moment as a tease, return to the beginning and then run until the end. A suspended interest structure works when the story is compelling enough to hook the reader. It worked for Time magazine in a story called "A Case of Mommie Dearest?"

> On a sunny afternoon last May, just two days before Mother's Day, a parcel arrived at the two-story brick home of Howard and Joan Kipp, in the Bay Ridge section of Brooklyn. The package was addressed to Joan, 54, a supervisor of guidance counselors in New York City's public schools. Standing in her kitchen, Mrs. Kipp tore off the brown wrapping paper and found the Quick and Delicious Gourmet Cookbook. She opened the cover. Suddenly there was a flash, and two .22-cal. bullets tore into her chest. Kipp came running into the room and discovered his bleeding wife on the floor, gasping, "A bomb! A bomb!" Three hours later, she was dead.
>   The bomb had been rigged up ingeniously. The cookbook was only 1½ in. thick, but someone had hollowed it out and placed inside a six-volt battery wired to gun-

powder and three bullets. The police were mystified, as were neighbors and co-workers. Who would want to do Mrs. Kipp any harm? Affable and popular, mother of two grown children, Joan Kipp was treasurer of the Bay Ridge Community Council and was expected to be named vice president the following month. Said her grieving son Craig, 27, to a group of reporters: "It was an irresponsible, violent act that doesn't make any sense at all."

Worse to come? Inside the boobytrapped book was scrawled an ominous note: DEAR HOWARD, YOUR DEAD/ BUT FIRST JOAN/ CRAIG NEXT/ DOREEN TOO/ NO MORE GAMES. The police immediately began guarding the entire family. Since the bomb went through the mail, a federal crime, an investigation was mounted by agents of the U.S. Postal Inspection Service. Said one inspector: "It took a lot of thinking to make that bomb."

By early summer they had quizzed some 200 people. Then, finally, a break: a handwriting expert matched the printing in the book's message to that of one of the suspects. The police subpoenaed a sock belonging to the suspect and let a trained German shepherd sniff it; the dog was then set loose in a room containing the remains of the real bomb and four replicas. The animal headed straight for the genuine one, and the sock owner's scent. Last week, 91 days after Mother's Day, police arrested their suspect outside his Brooklyn apartment and charged him with mailing the deadly package—to his mom. The accused: Craig Kipp. The motive of Kipp, an unemployed marine engineer, was not known. Craig's father, for one, stoutly proclaimed his son's innocence, and raised the money to pay the $300,000 bail.

Sometimes, of course, it is possible to write a suspended interest, or pure chronology, of an event in which the outcome is widely known. Saul Pett recapped the fall of Richard Nixon, H.G. Bissinger recreated the events through the 44 seconds in which an airplane with 89 people aboard plummeted 34,000 feet, and David Hacker recreated the last day of the four couples who were at the Hyatt Regency the night the skywalks collapsed. In each case, the outcome was known, but the detailed reporting and the magnitude of the event was dramatic enough to engage readers. In those cases even writers feel the excitement. Wrote Hacker of his Hyatt story, "I could feel the drama building as I wrote on, hour after hour, even though I knew, and I knew that the reader would know, what the outcome would be." Dramatic stories tell themselves; the suspended interest structure is appropriate. Those stories come to most writers only once or twice in a career. That's why it is important to know the other story structures and when to use them.

What we have presented here are guideposts, not straitjackets. Accomplished writers chart their own course, find new routes. The rest of us are thankful for a map. You have to travel the route a few times before you start noticing the sideroads.

6

writing the long story, the investigative story, the funny story

Saul Pett recalls from an otherwise-forgotten play a line that suggests both the fascination and the frustration of his craft: "Writing isn't hard; thinking is hard."

This chapter is about three varieties of writing that demand particularly hard thinking because of the special problems they generate. The three are writing at length, writing the investigation and writing with humor.

Although each kind of story—like any other kind—poses its own puzzles that you'll have to solve, the demand they have in common is their requirement of discipline. Each requires planning and organization. Each forces you to make that most painful of a writer's decisions: the decision to leave out much of the material you have so painstakingly accumulated. If your reporting has been good, you'll have a lot to leave out. This chapter will help you make those choices.

Discipline makes an even more basic demand. "When you're writing, it's important to keep your feet still," observes Washington Post writer Thomas Boswell. "There's too much desire to walk around the room, avoid the story, to try to find a wonderful outline, to go back and reresearch things for the 85th time, to fill out file cards—all because you don't want to face the actual task of writing. Sometimes you simply have to put your feet down and start writing."

THE LONG STORY

We'll start with the special problems of long stories. Newspapers, magazines and organization publications all often use pieces of 1,500 words or more. In magazines, especially, articles of 10,000 words are not uncommon. Whatever the medium, the principles of good writing apply.

Such principles as clarity and coherence are most easily lost, and discipline is most important, when you are writing at length. The sheer volume of your raw material—stacks of notes, tapes of interviews, copies of documents, volumes of background reading—can be overwhelming. The complexity of your subject—a reconstruction of the eruption of Mount St. Helens, an investigation of a state juvenile justice system, a word portrait of a public figure—can be paralyzing. The blank sheet of paper in your typewriter, the cursor blinking in the upper-left-hand corner of an empty VDT screen can drive you to consider seeking work as a school bus driver. But deadline approaches. What's an overburdened writer to do?

First, sit still. Then organize.

The hardest part and the most important part of writing any story is deciding its theme, deciding just what the story is. That decision guides all the writing that follows. The process of reaching that decision, and the accompanying process of organization, should begin long before you sit down before a keyboard.

Every experienced writer organizes, consciously or not, from the moment a story idea is born. The very expression of the idea implies the beginnings of organization. Your reporting will be guided—just as the writing will be at a later stage—by whether you are, for example, profiling Ed Koch as political leader of New York City or as the private man behind the public image. If you have reason to suspect corruption in a prison system or a welfare system, your whole approach to the story probably will be different from your approach if the idea is to describe how the system works.

The focus of a story often changes, of course, as reporting uncovers the unexpected. But the new focus will suggest its own working outline.

A good reporter is often likened to a vacuum cleaner, voraciously sucking in facts from desk tops and dark corners. The analogy is not perfect. A reporter whose fact-gathering is simply suction will wind up with a bag full of junk, the useful information buried in debris. A vacuum cleaner is not concerned with relevance. A reporter must define relevance broadly, trying to learn everything that may be of use and trying not to overlook any fruitful source. But the test of relevance must be applied.

Organizing as you report serves two purposes. It improves the efficiency of the reporting, saves time and helps you guard against oversight. It also simplifies the next step—organizing the writing. Difficult as you may find the job of sorting a story from the raw material of your reporting, the job will be vastly more difficult if your reporting has lacked the discipline of organization.

Still, in order to be sure that you have what you need, you will accumulate much more than you can use. Experienced writers usually use outlines of some sort to reduce that mass to manageable proportions.

Gaylord Shaw won a Pulitzer Prize for his Los Angeles Times stories on dam safety. The topic was massive and complex. To handle it and other major projects, Shaw uses an outline to break his information into "chunks"—each chunk being a subtopic. He has trained himself to write the sections separately, linking them later with transitions. Others prefer to write straight through from beginning to end, but they organize, too.

Richard Zahler of the Seattle Times won the writing competition sponsored by the American Society of Newspaper Editors for his recreation of the Mount St. Helens eruption. In the anthology *Best Newspaper Writing 1981*, he tells how he organized:

> I riffled through a stack of notes like a deck of cards. It was all in one big pile, but I had it so I could peel through it as I needed after I made an outline. I did the outline first. I knew what material was there. I knew whose stories I had. The outline was no more than: Intro (yet to be written), Geology becomes the second section, next something like Eruption History. Then it gets into individual stories of what happened on the day of the eruption. . . .

That may strike you as dull, mechanical work, but it is essential. And it doesn't have to be dull.

You can use the act of outlining—whether you are physically separating notebooks into piles, shuffling notes like cards, or drafting a formal outline as you were taught to do in elementary school—as part of the creative process.

As you sort your material, you can pick the quotes and anecdotes that illustrate or support each subheading of the outline. You can spot any holes in your reporting. Organizing, especially if you use a formal outline, should force you to come to grips with ambiguities or uncertainties that may still stand between you and a real understanding of some key point. Perhaps most important, outlining allows you to decide what to leave out.

The painful decision to leave out a good quote, a delightful anecdote, a hard-earned fact is a decision that too many writers avoid. Their avoidance burdens either an editor, who is forced to make choices the writer should have made, or a reader, who is faced with redundancy.

An outline, especially a formal outline, makes it much easier for you to see how much is too much. Three quotes that carry the same message or two anecdotes with similar points may each appear unique scattered through your notes. Their repetitiveness is revealed when they are clustered under the discipline of an outline.

As a reporter, you have to collect every quote, anecdote or fact that seems even remotely relevant in order to come as close as possible to the truth. As a writer, you risk obscuring the truth if you dump, undigested, too much of your collection onto your readers. Just as you break up your material into manageable chunks by outlining before you write, so you need to help your readers by break-ing your longest stories into readable chunks. Usually the best way to do that is either to make the chunks of roughly equal substance and run them as a series or to tell the main story in one chunk and break off subsidiary elements into sidebars.

A series is usually best if:

> The amount of information you want to convey is too much for a single story of reasonable length;
> You have several elements of roughly equal importance to anchor each installment in the series;
> You want to keep your subject in the public eye for longer than just one reading.

Reasonable people, to say nothing of unreasonable people such as writers and editors, can disagree about what is a "reasonable length." The worst way to settle the argument is by the imposition of arbitrary limits. A reasonable length for one story may be 6 inches and for another 60 inches. One flexible but usable guideline is this: When a story looks long to you, think of the poor reader and look for ways to break it up. Good editors will welcome, though they won't al-ways adopt, writers' suggestions on story treatment.

Once the decision is made to tell a story in multiple parts, the most impor-tant question is whether a series can be sustained. You should not start readers off with a blockbuster of a first story and follow with a string of much weaker subsid-iary stories. Those should be treated as sidebars instead of chapters in a series. Each story in a good series has substance enough to stand on its own, while being clearly identified as part of a greater whole.

Donald Barlett and James Steele, in their Philadelphia Inquirer "Energy Anarchy" series, led off with an overview piece that set out their theme: ". . . the schizophrenic division between what politicians say the federal government is do-ing about energy and what really is happening further obscures a crisis that al-ready promises to be the most persistent and pervasive the nation will face in the decade of the 1980s—energy anarchy."

The following installments each examined in detail one element in the an-archy. Part One, for example, was headlined, "The more we use, the more we have." Part Six told "How the oil industry is monopolizing energy." The result: manageable chapters of a story totaling more than 30,000 words.

Sometimes the divisions are obvious. Ken Fuson wrote in the Columbia Daily Tribune of the impact of cancer on child victims and their families. His introduction explained both the story and its structure:

> Hope powers the soul of children with cancer.
> How depressing, we think of those children. How depressing we think that way—blind to a side of the human spirit not even cancer can touch.
> For four days, the Tribune will profile youngsters treated at the only facility in Mid-Missouri that specializes in childhood cancer.

> The stories of Kitty Derr, Danny Chapman, Jeff Blatchford and Mark Spencer are not unlike those of the 6,100 youngsters diagnosed with cancer each year.
>
> Their lives are daily struggles to cope with a disease that remains a mystery. Their families, caught in a web of uncertainty, seek an all-too-elusive return to normal. And the health professionals who care for them see cancer's two faces: the promise of healthy futures and the pain of futures lost.
>
> These stories are about life. And where there's life, there's hope. . . .

Each story in Fuson's series was identified for readers with the same typographic signature, a shaded block with the headline in all capital letters, "THE UNDAUNTED," and a subhead, "Youth coping with cancer." Each block then identified the installment ("Part Three") and described it briefly, with a small picture of the child featured.

The trick is to identify each installment for those readers who are following the series while still making each appealing enough to attract a first-time reader. Some editors prefer to downplay the series identification for fear of scaring away readers who either missed a previous chapter and might not want to plunge into the middle of something or those wary of massive stories. Whether the linkage is bold or subtle, each installment in a series should contain a paragraph or two making clear how this piece fits into the whole.

Decisions on the packaging and display of stories are not, of course, usually made by the writers. Still, as a writer, you need to be aware of the possible pitfalls. Your name, not the editor's, will appear on the stories whether they are displayed well or badly and no matter whether their presentation helps or confuses the reader. By knowing what the considerations are, you may be able to influence the outcome to your and the reader's benefit.

Those at both ends of the communication process often can benefit from that other common organizational tool, the sidebar. Sidebars help writers simplify and clarify complex subjects. They help readers digest otherwise-unpalatable chunks of information. Sidebars can be used instead of or in conjunction with installments in a series.

Three reporters for the Fort Worth (Tex.) Star-Telegram spent most of a year researching the emergence of the information industry as America's most important. The reporters' work was published in a week-long series. Each installment had several sidebars.

One, repeated several times, was a glossary of industry jargon. Entries ranged from the merely uncommon ("WORD PROCESSING—A computerized method for typing and editing text [words.]") to the esoteric ("COMPUNICATIONS—Information industry jargon for technologies that merge the advancements in microelectronics and telecommunications to create computerized communication devices, products and services.") Had it not been for that device, which could be used in many other situations as well, the terms either would have remained undefined or would have had to be explained parenthetically in the body of a story already crammed with heavy material.

The Star-Telegram also used sidebars to elaborate on elements that could only be introduced in a main story of manageable length. For example, with a story on entrepreneurs in the new information age, reporters Tom Steinert-Threl-keld and Gerry Barker produced sidebars highlighting such disparate examples as Xerox, a giant trying to adapt, and a little company called Artificial Intelligence Corp., which has produced a computer language using plain English.

Sidebars can be used to emphasize the humanity that might otherwise be lost in a massive analysis or investigation. Here is a good example of that use in a prize-winning Detroit News expose of laxity and wrongdoing in Michigan's system of appeals from criminal convictions. Notice particularly how in their fifth paragraph, writers Norman Sinclair and Fred Girard linked the sidebar to the central theme of the major story.

> Six years have slowly passed since the prison gates first closed behind Edmond Green.
> He was 18 at the time, and he was scared.
> He admits to being wild. He knew nothing about the law.
> Now, having passed his 24th birthday in prison, he says he's a lot smarter—about the law, his rights, and the system he feels abused him.
> In examining more than 1,000 files of appeals for indigents in the Michigan Court of Appeals, The Detroit News found an array of pitfalls and loopholes in the system—unnecessary delays, court errors, lack of attorney-client communication, attorney swapping, improper billing, and others—and Green's case seemed to suffer from every one. . . .

Sinclair's and Girard's main story was long and complex, heavy with the statistics necessary to support their strong conclusions. The first two paragraphs give a good idea of its tone:

> Publicly paid lawyers, through carelessness or incompetence, are undermining the constitutional right of appeal of needy defendants in Michigan.
> Each year, up to 3,000 defendants—all of them poor, most of them uneducated—face an odds-against roll of the dice with their legal right to appeal. The odds are against them because of their court-appointed attorneys and the suspect system in which they operate. . . .

Edmond Green was a victim of that system. In the main story, he might have gotten as lost as in the Michigan court system. In a sidebar, his tragedy is inescapable.

Clarity is the prime virtue in journalistic writing. Careful organization, including the use of an outline and the dividing of long pieces into series or sidebars, makes clarity possible. Simplicity of writing style assures it. A good guideline is: The more complicated the subject, the simpler should be the style.

Let's go back to the Star-Telegram series on the information industry. The topic is almost incredibly complex. The industry is huge, new and secretive. Its processes are sophisticated, its language arcane. The reporters' findings required 37 stories for the telling.

Tom Steinert-Threlkeld's lead on the first story was simply, "You can't eat information."

He continued:

> It is intangible. Invisible. Its true nature is energy stored in our brain cells. It is neither fact nor idea nor the act of knowing, but the communication of knowledge, of facts and ideas. It is a series of impulses that travels through our body's nerve networks, then is emitted through such "output" devices as our mouth, eyes or hands. . . .

For two more simply worded paragraphs, he described the processes by which information has been transmitted. Then, with the scene set, comes the transition to the point of the series:

> We are on the threshold of an information revolution that will determine more about the way we live, work and play than anything that has come before. The information revolution will bring more change than the industrial revolution—perhaps even influence the balance of world power as electronics-controlled services increasingly replace petroleum-based products.
>
> The industry behind the creating, transmission and marketing of information is becoming—if it hasn't already—the largest portion of our economy. Larger than automobiles, larger than steel, larger than agriculture.
>
> Yet it too, in the public mind, remains largely invisible. . . .

A complicated story is introduced simply and told clearly.

Stories told with humanity as well as simplicity are even more likely to be interesting and entertaining. Sociology, the study of human societies, is largely unknown territory to non-specialists because of the jargon and statistics in which its findings are usually couched. The Los Angeles Times set out to explain an ominous phenomenon familiar to scholars but not the public—the growth of a permanent American underclass. The statistics show that millions of the perpetually poor are costing the rest of society at least $30 billion a year. The statistics are dull. The poor are not. Gaylord Shaw and David Treadwell began their story:

> CHICAGO—On a slate-gray morning in late May, Louise Loman stepped through the newspapers blown along the sidewalk, entered a grime-streaked office building and climbed the worn marble staircase to the waiting room of the state Public Aid Department.
>
> Beside her, matching her measured tread, was her 19-year-old daughter, Teresa. Cradled in Teresa's arms, wrapped snugly in a sparkling white blanket against the morning chill, was the teenager's month-old baby, John.
>
> They mounted the staircase in silence, each with her own thoughts.
>
> Louise Loman, 57, had been on welfare for 35 consecutive years, so a trip to the welfare office was nothing new to her. But this morning was different. This morning, the process would begin to place baby John's name on the nation's welfare rolls. He

would represent the third successive generation in the Loman family to receive welfare. . . .

Statistics showed that there was a story worth telling. People make it a story worth reading. And these are real people, not hypothetical cases or composites. The names were changed, but the reporters walked that sidewalk, climbed those stairs and got to know Louise Loman's family. How well and how the Lomans fit into the social class they personify begin to be revealed in the next few paragraphs:

> The Lomans' path to the welfare office was paved, in part, by problems of their own making, not least among them the seven of Louise's 10 children who were born out of wedlock and raised without the stability traditionally associated with a two-parent household.
> But forces beyond this family's control were also involved: forces great enough to overwhelm perhaps even the most determined individual.
> Increasingly, a number of economic, demographic and social forces has converged on members of the Loman family and millions of others like them, overwhelming their meager resources and locking them in the nation's economic and social basement. They are members of what appears more and more to be a permanent underclass in America. . . .

The Loman family brings to life the two full newspaper pages required for a story that was itself only part of a larger project. The sense of hopelessness that permeates the underclass and the story is articulated by one Loman son, Dennis, 20, in the soliloquy that closes the story:

> "You get out there, trying to find something," Dennis said. "But it don't get no better. They say, 'Call you in two weeks,' but you never get that phone call.
> "I need a job, man. That's what's happening in my life. A job."

It is a long story, but is is palatable. It is simply and humanly told.

The theme that runs through the story of the Loman family is hopelessness. It is introduced in the dreariness of the opening scene; it echoes in the penultimate paragraph. Repeated in quotes and descriptions throughout the story, it is a unifying element. Long and complicated stories, however logical their organization and graceful their style, need that recurring character or image to keep the reader from going astray. Well done, such repetition can set the tone for the story, much as the bass player in a jazz band lays down the rhythm from which the horn players improvise.

You can see the theme-setting work in these excerpts from William Nack's *Sports Illustrated* profile of chess prodigy Yasser Seirawan. The second paragraph introduces it:

> Whenever the squeeze was on, Yasser Seirawan found an escape, whether by someone else's hands or his own—from Syria to England to the U.S.; from the loneliness of gray Seattle days to the camaraderie of chess; from borderline poverty to Euro-

pean hotels with brass doorknobs; in one short leap from childhood to an adult world of university coffeehouses; from high school to life on the road as a chess junkie and hustler; and from the obscurity of an aspiring chess champion to the measure of fame accorded only those at the very top of the game. . . .

Only two paragraphs later, the theme is elaborated:

To the extent that chess can serve as a metaphor, Seirawan is a knight, the only piece on the board that avoids danger or attacks by sailing over and around a threat or an obstacle. . . .

A dozen paragraphs later, a slight variation on the theme:

His discovery of chess, the central event in his episodic life, was a consequence of the dramatic change in weather he experienced when he moved with his mother from coastal Virginia back to the Pacific Northwest. . . .

Two pages later:

High school had become a confinement, keeping him too long in Seattle. There were tournaments to play and places to go. So he left the chess team he had created, took the class princess, Marlene Williams, to the junior prom and was off to queen his pawn. . . .

A page later:

Right out of high school, he traveled to New York to make a killing. Dressed in safari shorts with 12 pockets and a tank top decorated with spider webs, he swooped down on Times Square—the Seattle Kid disguised as a surfer. . . .

And finally, in the story's last paragraph, a quote from his mother that sounds the unifying theme again, summing up:

"It's not strange that Yasser's with Korchnoi," she said while the match was still on. "He's being groomed to do this. He's looking them in the eye right now. . . . At 21, Yasser's right under Karpov's nose. You don't think he's learning? He's watching, you know. That's what chess is all about, going deeper and deeper, at all levels."

Nack's is a long piece, rich in detail and packed with anecdote. But he continually, subtly reminds his reader what the story is really about—Seirawan the knight, living his game. The key to successfully using such a unifying element is the key to writing any long story. That is deciding what the story *is*. Once the crucial decision is made, the rest isn't easy, but it is possible. With clarity as your goal, let your readers know early what you're telling them and why. Then remind them from time to time.

If your long story is a pure narrative, beginning at the beginning and recreating events in the order in which they happened, you can introduce your theme and let it evolve with the unfolding of the tale. That is Nack's approach. But many stories don't lend themselves to narrative rendition. Analytical and investigative stories, especially, need a section near the top in which you lay out in summary form the gist of the story.

The lead lures the customers into the tent, the body of the story provides the facts and the humanity to dazzle and amaze, the ending sends them home satisfied. The summary section stands between lead and body, justifying the barker's pitch and telling the still-skeptical onlookers the meaning of what they're about to see.

Tom Duffy, longtime teacher of writing at the Missouri School of Journalism, liked to call the summary section the "fat paragraph." He wanted it bulging with the conclusions drawn from the feast of facts that followed.

In Chapter 5, we called it the theme paragraph. Some call it the "nut" paragraph, because it contains the kernel, the meat of the story.

By any name, it is an important part of many long stories. And most of the stories that don't have the theme paragraph would be better if they did.

Robert Howard won a national award for his investigative reporting on company-sanctioned drug use within AT&T. His story for Mother Jones magazine began with a series of anecdotes illustrating the scope of the problem. Then he told his readers what it all meant:

> There is, to be blunt, a stress epidemic at AT&T. A four-month investigation by Mother Jones has revealed that incessant oversupervision, automatic computer monitoring, elaborate productivity indexes and petty management rules have made job-related stress pervasive at the 23 operating companies of the Bell system.
>
> And whether they receive tranquilizers from their own doctor or from their employer, more and more telephone workers have turned to drugs to put the lid on that stress. The situation has gotten so bad that even Ma Bell is concerned. A recent corporation-wide work relationship survey found that nearly half of the 50,000 respondents—from the lowliest operator to the highest-level manager—felt that stress on the job is worse than ever before. . . .

He goes from there to support his conclusions with statistics and anecdotes from a variety of sources. Mother Jones is a journal with a well-defined point of view. Its writers generally view the world from the perspective of the Left. That does not relieve them, however, of the burden any reputable journalist carries, the burden of supporting conclusions with facts.

Saul Pett writes for that quintessentially middle-of-the-road organization, the Associated Press. His language doesn't carry the bite of a Mother Jones article. But his fat paragraphs are just as well-nourished. He began a description of Fort Knox by introducing its supervisor, George Wright. Then the nut of it:

> To tell it straight out, there are 147,342,320.272 ounces of gold at Fort Knox, more than was ever viewed by all the pharaohs of Egypt or the conquistadors of Spain, or the Hunts of Texas. George Wright is responsible for every ounce and fraction thereof.

> This is Uncle Sam's largest single hoard, more than half the total gold stashed around the country by the government. At the peak of the market in January, the local stuff alone was worth more than $123 billion. There is no law that says it can't be sold. It is no longer needed to back up our currency. If sold, it conceivably could wipe out the federal deficit for years. . . .

More important than the style that distinguishes them is the substance that these two summaries have in common. Both tell their readers, in clear and simple terms, what the stories are about. Both are composed of unqualified assertions. Neither bears any attribution. Both follow anecdotal leads and introduce lengthy, fact-filled bodies. Both summarize both the substance and the tone of the stories that surround them.

The theme paragraph is an exercise in discipline. But then, so is nearly the whole art of writing at length.

WRITING THE INVESTIGATION

The challenge of writing an investigative piece has much in common with any writing at length. The same problems of organization, discipline, structure and helping the reader along must be overcome whether your story is investigative, analytical or descriptive. But the writer of investigative stories faces some complications that are less common, and sometimes unknown, in other forms of journalism.

> The substance of an investigation is often heavy going. Many important investigative stories are based on contract specifications, computer analyses, travel vouchers, telephone records and other details with little intrinsic reader interest.
>
> The threat of challenges, by lawsuit or by public relations counterattack, is always present. The prose of a feature writer is seldom scrutinized by the company lawyer; the investigative reporter's writing must be able to sustain such scrutiny.
>
> The burdens of fairness and balance are never heavier than when your story will damage reputations or careers.

The final requirement of any story is that it be read. If you are to expose an evil, right a wrong or accomplish any other worthy end, you have to get the customers into your tent and keep them there. That's why the best investigative reporters and editors today bring to their work the same sharp-eyed observation, the same precise crafting of the language that all good writers employ.

We've already looked at some of Gaylord Shaw's work. Like many of his colleagues, he prefers to use anecdotal leads on his investigative stories rather than the stodgy "The Los Angeles Times has learned. . . ." approach that is more traditional.

"You've got to sort of lure the reader in," he advises. There are in writing as in bass fishing a great variety of lures. The lure of humanity in the person of

Louise Loman introduces the unsuspecting reader to the American underclass. Philadelphia Inquirer reporter Ric Tulsky used human tragedy to interest readers in an investigation of a mass transit system, a subject that had the potential for a story as deadly dull as the system was deadly.

> Melvin Young lost his life boarding a train. With his foot caught in the door of a crowded subway car, he was dragged down the 15th Street station platform into the tunnel and killed.
> William McDowell lost his right eye driving a bus. The brake pedal fell off and lay like a broken toy on the floorboard while McDowell's bus, unable to stop, rearended an Audi and then a Chrysler on City Line Avenue, then jumped a curb and rammed a tree.
> Bertha Pressley was luckier. All she lost was several months' pay after being injured when the bus she was riding collided with a car. But as a result, Mrs. Pressley fell behind on her house payments and other bills and couldn't send her teenage children to the prom.
> These three people are victims of the Southeastern Pennsylvania Transportation Authority (SEPTA), the nation's third largest transit system. They are three among thousands. . . .

Notice the ominously alliterative cadence of the last line. It hints of even greater horror to come. Notice the specifics, the details. Good reporting is being put to the service of good writing.

Shaw's and Tulsky's are anecdotal leads. They work. Usually, this kind of story-telling approach is the best lure into a story that is hard and heavy. Readers aren't bass, though. You can't just set the hook and reel them in. The writer's lure must be an integral part of the story, not a deceptive adornment.

Shaw told his sociological tale through the Loman family from start to finish. Similarly, Tulsky's story of neglect, decay and danger is packed with vivid imagery and full of people all the way through. Riders complain that subway stations "are dreary and reek with the smell of urine." Readers meet trolley driver Ken Tomczuk, whose brakes failed on a hill. "Result: 21 people taken to hospitals, one of them unconscious." And 74-year-old Helen Creedon, a bus passenger in another crash. "Result: five people taken to the hospital, including Mrs. Creedon and her 72-year-old husband, Francis."

This is detail that enlivens and advances the story rather than encumbering it.

Sometimes, more rarely, your material will lend itself to a hard, summary-lead approach. Most investigative reporters and editors probably would agree with the late editor and teacher Paul Williams' criteria for deciding when the hard lead is best. Use a hard lead, he says, only if:

> There is a single, overwhelming revelation to be made;
> The context is already familiar to the average reader;
> The evidence supporting the lead is unequivocal;
> The story is simple enough to have few subplots and to need no chronology.

The Detroit News series by Sinclair and Girard was long (the reprints fills 16 tabloid pages) and loaded with detail, but the central theme is chillingly simple. The hard lead works:

> Publicly paid lawyers, through careless or incompetence, are undermining the constitutional right of appeal of needy defendants in Michigan. . . .

The evidence that supports the flat assertion is voluminous and persuasive.

Here is another hard lead that almost demands the reader's attention. It is from a Kansas City Times sports investigation.

> WICHITA—The Wichita State University Shockers, an emerging basketball powerhouse, are one of the best teams money can buy.
>   Several of the team's recent basketball players have told the Kansas City Times that they received thousands of dollars in cash, clothes, airline tickets and "forgiven" loans during the last three years from coaches and wealthy team boosters. . . .

That is about as clearly and strongly as you could start a story. The first paragraph is what a lawyer would call libel per se, libel on its face. It is not a paragraph to be written if you harbor the slightest doubt that you could defend it in court. There has been no indication that the Times will have to do so.

The Times story—written by Knut Royce, Richard Serrano and Mike DeArmond—goes on quickly to perform another service for its readers. The writers include three theme paragraphs to tell the readers what it all means:

> The investigation uncovered practices that appear to violate National Collegiate Athletic Association rules governing college sports at member institutions.
>   In Wichita State's case, amateurism was dealt a setback, and it was done in style. Plane tickets, according to the athletes, were front-cabin, the wardrobe was cut of the finest cloth, and the cash was $100 bills so crisp that they were hard to separate. Such gratuities violate NCAA rules banning certain forms of financial assistance not available to all students.
>   Boosters or alumni who give money or provide services to athletes are not themselves in violation of NCAA rules. An athlete violates the rules through the acceptance of such services, and a school violates the rules if its officials are aware of the athlete's acceptance. . . .

Too many investigative reporters are content to marshal their findings and parade them across a page without ever summing up, without taking the step of making clear the significance of those findings. This failure to get to the point—usually defended as "letting the readers draw their own conclusions"—is really an abdication of the writer's first duty: to be clear.

Detail must be used to support the point of an investigative story, not allowed to obscure it. The point sometimes will be that the situation itself is confused and unclear. An important part of the journalist's craft is the ability to write clearly about confusion. Every investigative story worth publishing has a point, maybe more than one. You owe your readers the same service the Kansas City Times reporters performed for theirs.

Another virtue of the Times story is that it doesn't go on forever. It runs only about 50 inches, with a sidebar of about 30 inches. Many investigative pieces consume three or four times that space. Sometimes, of course, the material demands great length. When it does, a series or multiple sidebars is usually the best format. But in many cases, investigative pieces run on and on and on because the writer, the editor or the company lawyer feels compelled to display every shred of evidence and use every quote from every witness. The compulsion is understandable, but you should resist it.

Your obligation as a writer is to tell the readers what you've found and what it means. Then you should provide enough evidence to show that your conclusions are well-founded, but no more. If, as is often the case, you have 10 examples, use two and just tell the readers you have more. If the two really show what you say they do, readers will believe you. And they probably will thank you for your restraint. Similarly, if you have three or four human sources saying essentially the same things, print only the best. Save the rest.

Especially in these litigation-happy times, it will be a great comfort to you and your lawyer to know there's more where the examples you've printed came from. Being able to demonstrate that you've shown restraint should also be helpful when an opposing lawyer starts inquiring into your state of mind, as the courts now allow. It will be much more difficult for the other side to show malice if you can truthfully point out that you dug up even more evidence than you published.

The appearance and the reality of fairness, of balance, are just as important in establishing credibility with readers as they are in protecting yourself against lawsuits.

"Harsh stories turn off readers," says Gaylord Shaw. His story on the underclass portrays the Loman family honestly but sympathetically. Avoiding harshness is particularly desirable in stories that have the effect of accusing someone of wrongdoing. In an investigation, after establishing that his target is a rotten crook, Shaw used what on the L.A. Times is called the "to be sure" paragraph, as in, "To be sure, the world is full of rotten crooks."

A slightly different approach serves the same end in the sidebar to the Kansas City Times' Wichita State story. The sidebar traces the remarkable improvement in living standard of the previously poverty-ridden family of a star player who accepted a scholarship to Wichita State. Purchases of a $62,500 home and a new car are among the improvements. The writers introduce the player's mother:

> Today Mrs. Carr is working at the Boeing Co. on the day shift as a dispatch clerk, "keeping parts moving from one shop to another," she said, "and keeping a record of where the parts are moving, clocking them by computer."
> She's still got problems. There's a bad right ankle and a bad back. But, all in all, she said, she can't complain.

The story then describes Mrs. Carr and her son Antoine, the star:

> Jo Ann Carr is an imposing, personable woman who stands 5 feet 11 inches tall. "My father was 6-6; my mother was 6 feet," Mrs. Carr said.
>
> Antoine, whom Mrs. Carr is wont to call "my baby" is a premier forward and is himself imposing at 6-feet-9. "Tall genes," Mrs. Carr said with a chuckle. . . .

Mrs. Carr also is given ample space to explain her version of the acquisitions. The overall impression left by the story is that improprieties have been committed. But the writers' fairness is equally evident. And the story radiates the warmth of humanity.

Fairness requires not only that you give your target a chance to respond to your findings but that you include any findings that are in the target's favor. From the Detroit News story on the state criminal appeals system:

> Of nearly 200 prisoners interviewed by The News, a few did feel the system had protected their rights.
>
> "I did the crime," one Jackson inmate said. "I copped (pleaded guilty); and the only reason I appealed was they told me I had a free one coming. I thought maybe they'd find some technicality or something.
>
> And a woman imprisoned at Huron Valley Women's Facility for second-degree murder said, "I got no complaints about my (appeals) lawyer. She tried hard, but there wasn't much she could do. I'm only doing 5½ years, and I deserve it. That's not much for taking a life."

The writers note the exceptions to the overall pattern, and they make clear that these are exceptions. It is clear, and it is fair. You owe your readers no less.

As these examples show, investigative writing can be good writing. You may have to work a little harder than in some other kinds of stories because of the special demands of investigative stories, but the principles of good writing apply universally.

WRITING WITH A LIGHT TOUCH

The Kansas City Times reporters in their investigation got a chuckle from Mrs. Carr. A chuckle is a rarity in an investigative piece; an honest-to-God belly laugh is a rarity in any journalism. That's too bad. If variety is the spice of life, humor is the honey of journalism, sweetening the usually dull and often bitter fare served up by most newspapers and magazines most of the time.

Humor can serve a writer well:

It can bring a person or a story to life;
It can convey even serious messages more palatably than can straight exposition;
It can provide a few minutes of plain, uncomplicated fun.

A light touch can be the right touch even in stories in which you wouldn't expect it. An obituary, for instance. When Henry Milander, a local legend who was the mayor of suburban Hialeah, died, The Miami Herald wrote in its front-page obituary:

> Once, in about the 29th year of his reign over Hialeah, several politicians were discussing Milander's remarkable hold on the mayor's office.
> Councilman Jack Weaver said, "He won't be around forever, but when he goes, he'll probably take the city with him."
> Henry himself told a reporter visiting City Hall, "The only way they'll get me out of here is shoot me."
> They didn't shoot him and he didn't take the city with him when he went Sunday, but the death of Henry Milander leaves a considerable void in the politics and the folklore of South Florida. . . .

Lightly but not flippantly written, the anecdote captures something of the style and the substance of its subject. That's just what a good obituary, or a good profile, should do.

Political analysis often is a test of a reader's endurance. Dennis Farney found a way to enliven while enlightening Wall Street Journal readers in a piece on political mavericks in Congress. His lead:

> WASHINGTON—One dreary afternoon, as the House of Representatives debated plant patents for hybrid okra, the tousle-haired figure of Rep. John Burton materialized to transform boredom into chaos.
> The San Francisco-area Democrat seized the microphone with a question—a serious one, he insisted. Might not the proposed changes in plant patent law lead to bureaucratic meddling in human reproduction?
> Not "unless the gentleman can extract a fetus from okra, celery, peppers, tomatoes, carrots or cucumbers," answered a nonplused Rep. E "Kika" de la Garza, the Texas Democrat who managed the legislation.
> "I could do that," Mr. Burton replied airily. "In fact, I have seen it done. It was in the gentleman's district."
> A fleeting expression crossed Mr. de la Garza's face. It was the expression of a man who stumbles into a nightclub act and, inexplicably, finds himself playing straight man in a comedy act. The irrepressible Mr. Burton moved on to a discussion of genetics. . . .

Both of these examples come from serious stories. Sometimes, though, the assignment is simply to entertain. Here's an excerpt from the story that resulted when a Miami Herald reporter revisited a kiddie matinee, accompanied by three children:

> One aspect of the matinee that was even more pronounced than I had remembered was the general state of stickiness. The matinee formula of popcorn, cola and chewing gum produces an emulsion on floors to make the Elmer's Glue people chartreuse with envy. And a four-year-old with a soft drink in one hand and a box of popcorn in the other is an unguided but parent-seeking missile.

The action at a Saturday matinee is not confined to the screen. Sometimes, the entire audience appeared to be in motion. At the least, half the patrons were bouncing in place. Near the end, a spirited game of hide-and-seek centered on our corner of the theater. (After the movie, the elder daughter, who is not a matinee regular, was asked the high spot of the show. "Going up and down the aisles in the dark," she replied.)

These segments from an obituary, a political analysis and a frothy entertainment piece have several things in common.

First, the humor in each emerges from the writer's applying the universal principles of good reporting. In each case, the key was close observation that yielded detail and anecdote. In the Milander obit, direct quotes are the key. Paraphrase would have been far less effective. In the politics story, a keen eye aided a good ear. John Burton is a "tousle-headed figure" speaking "airily." Rep. de la Garza appears "nonplussed" and wears a bemused expression that most readers will be able to imagine. In the matinee story, the exact ingredients of the "general state of stickiness" are specified, as is a familiar standard of comparison. The children are not just moving around; they are "bouncing in place" and playing hide-and-seek. In all three stories, the images are sharp, the description precise. Readers are given ample material from which to build the mental pictures that are essential to written humor.

Another important characteristic is that each excerpt is underwritten. The writers have avoided the common trap of trying to be cute. There is no fakery; no quotation marks used to call attention to "special" uses of words; no exclamation points; no stretching of the usual conventions of reporting and writing. Even in the first-person account, neither the writer nor the writing is intrusive.

The lesson of these examples is probably the single most important—and maybe the only—rule of effective humor writing in journalism: Find good material and underwrite it. Slapstick seldom works in print. If the substance is not funny, no typographical tricks, no verbal gymnastics will persuade a reader that it is. Print is a straight-faced medium. If you fail to respect its limitations, you risk being laughed at rather than laughed with.

There's another warning implied by the examples, too. At least some of you will not find them amusing. Humor is intensely individualistic. An anecdote that moves you to laughter may leave the person at the next desk unmoved at all. Humor writing is risky. That is another reason for writing humor with restraint. Those who agree with you that this is indeed funny will appreciate your subtlety. Those who disagree are likely to be at least less offended than if you had beaten them over the head with it.

Here are two more examples. The styles are sharply different, but both are humorous. We think they are, anyway. The first story is reprinted in its entirety:

Motley, Minn. (AP)—Sun flower seed shells are too light. Metal shot, accidentally swallowed, might cause gout. Olive pits are football-shaped and could dent spittoons.

So members of Sit'N'Spit International will again use cherry pits when they participate in the club's spitting classic during its annual convention next weekend.

Omar McGuire, president of the 300-member organization, said members will discuss whether to build a domed stadium in downtown Motley in case the City Hall isn't large enough for future spitting contests. The club also will take its annual tour of Morey's Fish Market, "just to have something else on the agenda. We believe there should be more foolishness in life," McGuire said.

Ridiculous facts are straight-forwardly reported. The humor lies in the situation, which is stripped of superfluous information and laid out in traditional wire service style. The writer has resisted every temptation to go too far. The result is a tiny gem.

Dave Barry, by contrast, writes in hyperbole. In this piece for the Philadelphia Inquirer, he consistently exaggerates for effect. His approach works, too.

Let's take just a quick look at the history of baby-having: For thousands of years, only women had babies. Primitive women would go off into primitive huts and groan and wail and sweat while other women hovered around. The primitive men stayed outside doing manly things, such as lifting heavy objects and spitting.

When the baby was born, the women would clean it up as best they could and show it to the men, who would spit appreciatively and head off to the forest to throw sharp sticks at small animals. If you had suggested to primitive men that they should actually watch women have babies, they would have laughed at you and probably tortured you for three or four days. They were real men. . . .

Outrageous assertions are all the funnier because they are stated simply, without unnecessary adornment. Barry then describes his participation, with his pregnant wife, in natural childbirth classes.

We saw lots of pictures. One evening, we saw a movie of a woman we didn't even know having a baby. I am serious. Some woman actually let some moviemakers film the whole thing. In color. She was from California. . . .

Short, simple sentences reinforce the pseudo-serious style. "She was from California" is certainly explanation enough of almost any aberrant behavior, at least to an audience of Philadelphians. He then discusses labor:

The woman goes through a series of what the medical community laughingly refers to as "contractions"; if it referred to them as "horrible pains that make you wonder why the hell you ever decided to get pregnant," people might stop having babies and the medical community would have to go into the major-appliance business. . . .

Medical jargon is turned deftly on its users. The contrast between euphemism and reality is a theme that runs through the story. Barry concludes:

All in all, I'd say it's not a bad way to reproduce, although I understand that some members of the flatworm family simply divide into two.

This sardonic tone is consistent throughout the piece. So is the use of surprising metaphors and comparisons. So is the understatement with which even exaggeration is delivered.

There is no formula for funny writing just as there is none for any other kind of good writing. There are, however, some useful guidelines.

Look closely and listen well to capture the nuances of description and phrasing that will permit you to show your readers something funny instead of having to try to persuade them that it is funny.

Strip your material of superfluous detail and unnecessary information. Focus on the point—the contrast, the absurdity, whatever it is that makes this funny. Provide just enough context to make the point clear.

Underwrite. Avoid tricky constructions, fake names, dialect or any other device that violates the conventions of the language. The humor must come from the material, from your ideas, from the use of legitimate literary devices such as metaphor and simile.

Finally, violate any of these guidelines if you can do so and be funny. True comic genius can make its own rules. These guidelines are just that—guides for any who need them. Those who don't are bound only by the ultimate rule: The reader must think it's funny.

7

specialized writing/organization publications

The wind blows constantly over parts of the Texas Panhandle. Sweeping dust under dried brush, it hurries over the barren plain as if tidying up after the human intruders.

These intruders are the exploration companies who come to play a gambler's game. They don't roll dice, spin wheels or shuffle cards. They shake the ground and drill holes, hoping to find natural gas and oil deep below the earth's parched, yellow cover.

Despite all the fancy technology, from seismic studies to satellite pictures, the exploration and production business remains a game of chance. The stakes are high, and Mother Nature has shaved the dice....

That's good writing. It didn't appear in a commercial newspaper or consumer magazine. It was written by Becky Christiansen for InterNorth, a corporation publication.

Good writing is often found in organization publications—but not often enough.

We choose the term "organization publications" because we mean to include government at all levels, the trade press, associations, business, corporations, offices of public information of hospitals, universities and other institutions.

Hundreds of thousands of publications keep bombarding people who take less time to read, have fewer reading skills and are increasingly skeptical about what they read. If you are a writer for an organization, you know that you are competing for the reading time of your audience. Probably you have little chance to compete with television. People read only so many minutes a day, and you are competing for that reading time against the best and the brightest publications out there.

You may have a slight advantage. People who belong to an organization or work for a company want and need to be informed. Take advantage of their special interest. Write as well as the best writers do. You are spending company dollars to buy time in today's hurry-up society. Every word counts. Good design and photography can enhance the message, but you must choose the words for that message—carefully.

Whether you write for an organization newsletter, magazine or brochure, what is important is that you write well. This chapter will help you do that. Because of the unique nature of specialized publications, we'll begin by discussing the purposes and content. Your appeal is different from other publications people buy. If you want to be read, you need to know what your specialized audience is interested in and adapt your style and approach to its needs.

We'll urge you to tell your organization's story through people, and we'll apply the principles of good writing to organization writing.

Most of all, we'll demonstrate that there are no dull subjects, only dull writing. Dull subjects are merely a bigger challenge for creative non-fiction writers, not millstones meant to drown you.

PURPOSES AND CONTENT
OF ORGANIZATION PUBLICATIONS

Good writing begins with knowing the organization you work for. What does it do? Who makes it happen? To whom does it happen?

Second, know your audience. Who are those people? What is their age and education? What do they do? What are their needs? You, like all magazine and newspaper editors, should conduct readership surveys. You should also give your readers space in your publication for questions, gripes or suggestions.

Third, you should know the purpose of each publication and of each article you write. Write out the purpose; there's no better way to know it.

The broad purposes of informing people haven't changed since Thomas Jefferson's time. Jefferson said that if people aren't told what is going on, only three possibilities exist: rumor, apathy or revolution. Rumor is seldom funny; often it's ugly, if not destructive. Rumors that a company is going bankrupt have caused it to go bankrupt.

Some wag has said most people aren't concerned about apathy, but organizations die and productivity declines as a result of it. Revolution manifests itself in many ways. Violence and sabotage have occurred in factories and in mines, and associations have disintegrated when leaders failed to communicate.

Communication must meet the needs of people, and the needs of people everywhere are much the same most of the time. The philosopher Nietzsche wrote that what people need to be human is a sense of security, a sense of accomplishment and a sense of recognition. Organization editors and writers would do well to remember those needs when deciding upon the objectives and subject matter of their publications. You must know the specialized needs of your specialized audience.

This is especially true for employee publications. What people most want to know about their work is how secure their jobs are. Company news is their chief interest because if the company is doing well, their jobs are secure, and the likelihood of raises and promotions is good.

For example, here's the lead in the lead story of a financial service corporation newsletter:

> December business resulted in the largest gain in consumer credit of any month in the company's history.

Nothing works like success, but success must be communicated if more is to come. News isn't always good, however, and just as certainly the organization editor must tell about financial problems and even impending layoffs and cutbacks. People may not like the truth, but they can deal with it much better than with rumor or uncertainty. And it's always better that they learn the truth from those with whom they are associated than from outside sources such as the daily newspaper.

At Inland Steel in East Chicago, Ind., there's a newsletter for all the newsletter editors of the various plants. When a rumor circulated that due to cutbacks newsletters would no longer be published, editor Don Yehle met it head-on:

> A rumor has been spreading that newsletters will be discontinued. "On the contrary, it's times like now that newsletters can and should be providing employees with information about the steel business," said Ron Pyke, director, Communications. "Employees are understandably concerned about their jobs, and they need to hear specific information pertaining to operations in their own departments."

When workers were laid off at the Johns-Manville Corporation, the lead story began:

> Adopting the methods of a custom tailor, the Pipe Division last month was forced to take in its seams and cinch its waistband to fit a lean national economy.
>
> A division "reorganization" became effective at the beginning of October which meant that several staffs were trimmed. Fifty employees at WHQ and in the Pipe Division's sales force were affected.
>
> The tailoring was necessary because, according to division general manager John Swensen, "with the economy the way it is, we had to reorganize to compete profitably in the market."

The story then goes on to discuss specifics and how the company would help those who were laid off. Editors of association publications also must enhance the sense of security of the members. After all, security is the main reason people join associations in the first place.

But there's more to life than security. Nietzsche also said people have to feel as if they're accomplishing something, as if they're doing something worthwhile. Organization publications have to report on the achievements of the organization and its members. These achievements must be related directly to the self-interest of the members or employees. Everyone wants to be a part of something, and usually a part of something that's doing things. You must learn what the organization is doing by cultivating sources and digging out the information.

Individuals in the organization like to feel as if they, too, are accomplishing something. They need someone to recognize their worth, their contributions. Employees indicate in surveys that they rank personal news far below company news, yet they often turn to personal news first. Editors know that readers want to see names of people and what they have done. Most of all they want to see their own names in the news. They like and need recognition. Some communicators make fun of the birthday, bowling and baby news, but this news has a place in organization publications. Editors who say readers are bored with such news are kidding themselves. Only the editors are bored.

Readers look for names and pictures of people—especially their own. When Archie Bunker was locked in his basement, convinced he was going to die, his son-in-law "the Meathead" asked him what he most regretted about his life. Without much hesitation, Archie said, "I never got my picture in the paper."

With costs of paper, printing and postage being what they are, editors have to decide whether they can afford to run Archie's picture. They have to decide how to communicate the organization's message in the most effective, efficient and economical way. Many organizations are choosing to cut costs and to cut reading time by publishing short, frequent newsletters. They are making a wise choice.

The newsletter contains, first of all, news. It says what's happening, and what's going to happen. If a newsletter is to have news, it must come out frequently. Members of an organization or employees of a corporation like to know what's going on, and they don't want to be the last to know. They also like frequent contact.

The newsletter is also a letter. It's short, friendly, conversational, informal. By being short, it says to the reader, "Read me now!" If the reader sets it aside for when there is time, chances are it will remain on that stack of good intentions until time for clean-up and the circular file. Too many newsletters are too long. In our big-is-better society, many editors have expanded their two- or four-page newsletters to eight or 12 pages. As a result, they have bigger publications but notably fewer readers.

Letters are personal and informal because you write them in the second person, and you use contractions. If you were writing a news story for a newspaper, you might write the lead this way:

> Employee Stock Ownership Plan (ESOP) participants will receive at least one extra card with their Sept. 29 paycheck.

Now the newsletter approach:

> If you're an Employee Stock Ownership Plan (ESOP) participant, you'll be receiving at least one extra card with your Sept. 29 paycheck.

Letters are written to individuals. A letter is not a mass medium. Don't write about employees in an employee newsletter; write to them. Instead of "Employees may apply for additional health benefits," write: "You may apply for additional health benefits."

Finally, to save money (and to show your readers that you are saving money), to demonstrate the urgency of the message (you didn't have time to get the copy set by a printer), and to appear more like a personal letter, you do well to set your newsletter in typewriter type. Better yet, if you have a good typewriter and a tight budget, type it yourself.

If your budget is bigger and you have the luxury of writing for an organization magazine, you have more space for better writing. In the magazine, as in the newsletter, your style should be personal, friendly and informal. But you have more space to tell the organization story, to fill in the background, to talk about goals and plans, to write about people's accomplishments.

TELLING YOUR STORY
THROUGH PEOPLE

In the organization magazine, you write for people best by writing about people. Any organization's story is the story of people, and in a magazine, you have the opportunity to tell us about those people.

For example, if you're writing about how well the city bus system can transport employees to work, you would do well to look for a person who regularly rides the bus to work. That's better than calling the officials or simply printing a schedule. If you look around you may find a Mary Koenig:

> "We've had some of the best bus drivers in the world," says Mary Koenig, bond department. "They are more than just our drivers—they're our friends."
> And that to Mary is just one of the many benefits reaped after 30 years of bus riding from her home in East St. Louis. She never did learn to drive and uses the bus for shopping and visiting, as well as transportation to and from her job.

Now you have an expert. You tell about the bus system in a human, interesting way, and you introduce Mary Koenig. Mary likes that, and so do the people who know her. Mary relates experiences she has had riding the bus, and before the story ends, you include the bus schedule.

You can also tell the story about a hospital through the people who work there. Some of those people aren't often seen, and few people know what they do. But without them, the hospital could not function. One story on a two-page picture spread in a hospital publication began this way:

> People depend on Bob Williams.
> For the past seven years, Bob has delivered supplies and linens to hospitals in Beaumont's Shared Services program. He makes daily runs to hospitals throughout Michigan's "thumb" area, and drives his 20-foot truck to Beaumont's warehouse in Traverse City.

The story accomplished two things: It told of an essential part of the hospital's operation, and it introduced us to one of the hospital's personnel, the person responsible for that essential part.

Tell your story, whether that's selling a machine or selling a service, through the people who have used or experienced it. When a telephone company decided to write about its newest digital switchboard system, it looked for people already using it. It found them in Busch Gardens. The story began this way:

> You are expecting 6,000 hungry guests for lunch, and at 10 a.m. you realize 15,000 are coming.
> You pick up the phone and are told you have five minutes to take the chairman of the board on a tour of The Congo.
> You discover on a routine inspection of your 300-plus acre plain that one of your prize giraffes is delivering two weeks early.

The story goes on to say why, in this hectic environment that demands immediate action, Busch Gardens selected the digital switchboard system.

Sometimes you write about people in your organization just for the fun of it. Perhaps they have unusual hobbies or an exceptional skill. Here's the beginning of a story with the delightful heading, "Bottle cap king searches for crowns."

> John Meyer's dedication to bottle caps runs deep.
> So deep that he dug a Dr. Mutch's root beer bottle cap out of a hot tar parking lot in Hershey, Penn., when he was 9 years old.
> Meyer, 28, thought he would outgrow his hobby.
> Instead, the hobby has grown to 1,026 lids. He has even built a display case to accommodate the Dr. Mutch's lid and the rest of the collection. And he's catalogued each cap.

The writer tells readers the kind of person Meyer really is. At one point he says, "I'd like to think I'm an enterprising guy trying to preserve a moment in history." It's a good people story.

GOOD WRITING

It also is good writing. Regardless of the medium, the writing is what counts. You must grab your readers, fight for every second of their time. And perhaps most of all in organization writing, you must write to be believed. Credibility is crucial. If you apply the characteristics of good writing as outlined in Chapter 5, you have a much better chance of being credible.

First, you must be correct. Be fanatical about spelling people's names correctly. Get the facts straight. Work out a system for checking your copy. Be grammatically correct at all times. This copy appeared on the front page of a corporation newsletter:

> Important to the success of each year's Arts Festival are corporate volunteers from Cleveland's business community. They sell programs, the proceeds of which help fund the annual event. They assist visitors with directions and information. They bring smiles to children by creatively decorating their faces with washable paint. And they have fun.

The copy is wordy and awkward, especially the second and third sentences. And readers of the publication will never know whether the corporate volunteers paint their own faces or those of the children.

The story would have been more interesting if it had focused on one corporate volunteer. At the least, it needed to be rewritten:

> Corporate volunteers from Cleveland's business community contribute each year to the success of the Arts Festival. They raise money by selling programs. They direct and inform visitors. They paint their faces and make children smile. And they have fun.

Readers may or may not have fun when they read this headline in a newsletter for a school system in Texas: "Cable TV On It's Way." There is no substitute for being correct.

Second, be consistent. Far too many organization publications have not adopted a stylebook. Editors abbreviate states in one story and not in another. They treat numbers in different ways at different times. They capitalize titles in one paragraph and boldface them in another.

Titles of people present special problems for organization editors. Whom do you call "Mr."? Do you use first or last names? Do you treat women's titles the same as men's? Do you use Miss, Mrs. or Ms?

There is no way that you can please everyone in these matters. But you can be consistent if you follow a stylebook, and readers will understand your need to be consistent.

Because you regularly deal with and write for the commercial press, you may as well adopt the Associated Press or United Press International stylebook.

Why should you risk the ire of newspaper copy editors by making them edit the copy to fit their style?

In addition, you'll need your own set of guidelines that covers your own situation. You'll have to decide how to refer to the company or to the chairman of the board. If you have several members on your staff or if your organization is spread out over different locations, you need a stylebook even more. After all, being inconsistent makes you appear incorrect. Consistency helps credibility.

You also need to be consistent in your approach to the story. A first-person story often works well. But if you write in the first person, jump into the story soon and stay in it. The same holds for the second person. Don't start out a piece writing about what employees may do and then address the reader directly with a "you."

Be consistent with the tense of the verb. Don't be afraid of the present tense, especially in profiles. But don't say "says" in one paragraph and "said" in another.

Be consistent in the tone or the mood of the story. Often leads are bright and exciting, only to be followed by dry, boring copy. The tone or mood of the piece is determined by the subject matter, the audience and the medium for which you are writing. You must decide on that mood before you start writing and stick with it throughout the piece.

Being consistent in all the ways we have mentioned also helps you to be more clear. All the other qualities of writing have no merit if the copy is unclear. Clarity is crucial for credibility. People know when you are trying to impress them, and they wonder why. Robert Gunning said write to express, not to impress. You express yourself best when you write simply, using simple words, simple sentences and simple paragraphs. A director of marketing research was not at his best when he wrote this:

> The proliferation of electronic media and sophisticated communications virtually ensures that we will be inundated with a sea of information in a variety of forms.

The same writer "facilitates" and "expedites" and "proselytizes" and "catalyzes," and then he "vis-a-vis" you. Beware of people who "vis-a-vis" you.

Beware also of people who write sentences like this in proposals:

> There is no space which can be called a *"Center"* to effectively establish a concept which is replete with potential for synergies.

Some of the muddiest copy is found in letters and memos where clarity and simplicity should be paramount. This is just part of a paragraph from a memo of a government official in British Columbia:

> In this regard it is important to make a clear distinction between the processes of handling afferent and efferent material. The efferent (out of uprouting) is to be processed as noted above. While it is desirable that each agent involved in the proc-

essing of incoming material should conform to the standard routing process, such incoming material does not have to conform to the flow configuration in that any subject, at the point of judgment and demand (Minister, Deputy Minister, Associate Deputy Minister, Director) may be chosen to pass directly to a specialty office.

That's only half the paragraph. The same official spells accommodate with one "m," and twice writes "its' " for "its."

You can improve clarity by being concise. Imagine that you are paying for it by the word. Imagine that you are paying your readers for every word they read.

This wordy draft of a brochure promoting a workshop for a state parks and recreation association would be costly:

> People are confronted today with a growing spectrum of leisure-time product and service alternatives. The consumer's choice of what goes into their leisure-time activities mix is influenced by many factors including relative cost, peer-group interests and preferences, and specific knowledge of the leisure-time opportunities available in their community.
>
> The objective of this seminar is to develop the marketing skills of professionals charged with the delivery of leisure services. Participants will learn how to better inform targeted clientele about their leisure programs and how to increase public knowledge and interest in these programs. In brief, you will learn how to market your community's or agency's leisure "product" more effectively.

The copy written more concisely is also more clear:

> People can choose from a growing number of things to do with their leisure time. Among the many factors that influence their choice are:
>
> >   relative cost
> >   peer-group interests and preferences
> >   specific knowledge of available leisure-time opportunities
>
> This seminar will teach you how to inform the public about your leisure programs and how to market them.

If you were buying space at a dollar a word, the second version would save you $53. There's also a good possibility that you would have more people at your seminar. It's not just that the copy is shorter. It's more concise, and hence, more clear.

Being coherent also helps clarity. Incoherence is the most serious failing of today's writers. As Marshall McLuhan wrote, people live in an electronic, nonlinear world where communication is more mosaic than it is sequential. But writing is linear and therefore must progress logically. You must take readers by the hand and lead them along: from word to word, sentence to sentence, paragraph to paragraph. Even the most experienced writers have to work at writing transitions.

Here is an example of a lack of transition in a Canadian government newsletter. A paragraph ends with this sentence:

> Today, having achieved world economic power, the city will become a centre of international sport, thanks to the Commonwealth Games and the new 42,500-seat Commonwealth stadium.
>   Bowls, also known as lawn bowling, is one of two sports seen at the Commonwealth Games, but not at the Olympics.

Readers need a bridge to get from the economic advantages of the games to lawn bowling. Here is one solution:

> The new stadium will host bowls or lawn bowling, a sport seen at the Commonwealth Games but not at the Olympics.

"The new stadium" is an overt reference to the previous paragraph. Here's another example from the same article. A paragraph ends:

> Such accomplishments have popularized track and field in Canada despite the short summer and the emphasis on team sports.
>   The Commonwealth Games stamps were designed by Stuart Ash of Toronto.

It needed a transition:

> Many of Canada's sports are now commemorated by the Commonwealth Games stamps, designed by Stuart Ash of Toronto.

Brevity at the expense of transitions is false economy. Good transitions often demand a repetition of key words in the previous paragraph. Make reading as easy as possible for your audience, regardless of who that audience is. Making your copy more understandable is also making it more credible.

However, one other element is necessary for credibility. You must tell the whole story whenever possible. You must be complete.

As an organization writer, this may be your biggest problem. Often you are told what you may or may not release. Horror stories abound about approval channels. In some areas, lawyers not only approve copy but also hand down the terminology writers must use. Everyone is an editor.

But if you are to be of any real worth to your organization, you must be the advocate of full disclosure, as soon as possible, or, at least, before your members or employees hear the news through rumor or from the daily press. For you, the communicator, the question is not *if* you are going to release the story, but *how* and *when*.

Sometimes being complete is merely doing your homework and having the facts, the specifics to back up your story. For example, a beer company would have been more effective in its story about the effects of a container deposit ordinance in a Midwestern city had it bothered to gather and write the convincing details. Here are a few paragraphs:

> If there is anything remotely humorous in the situation, it is the number of people who are so used to tab tops and twist off caps that they must call local retailers to ask how to get the caps off returnable bottles. At present, there is also a severe shortage of bottle openers and "church keys" in the city.
>
> The increased costs of transportation, delivery, storage and handling are shared by the consumer, and the result is soaring beverage prices. This has caused consumers and forced deposit proponents to cry "foul" because they failed to realize that business and consumers are partners in the market place.
>
> Many beer buyers have responded by going outside the city limits to purchase beer where they can select from a full variety of brands and packages, at significantly lower prices. . . .
>
> Grocery stores and liquor stores report a general loss of volume from people who are resistant to higher prices, housewives and older people who don't like to lug heavy cases of returnables, and beer drinkers who just prefer other packages and can get them outside the city.

The writer missed every opportunity to give concrete information that would have been much more convincing. In the first paragraph he talks in generalities about "a number of people" and of a "severe shortage." In the second paragraph he writes about "increased costs" and "soaring beverage prices" when he could very well have told us what they are. The second sentence of the second paragraph is an assumption.

With some research the writer could have reported how many beer buyers were going outside the city limits to purchase beer, and surely he could have found out what "significantly lower prices" and "a general loss of volume" were. If the writer had gone to one beverage dealer and told the story specifically and in depth, readers would have been more interested and more inclined to believe the writer. Because the story is incomplete, it is also less credible.

BEING CREATIVE

Credibility, then, comes from being correct, consistent, clear, concise, coherent and complete. But you can be all these things and still be boring. To compete for readers' time, your writing must be interesting and informative. To be that, it must be creative—original in thought and original in expression.

Here's where the fun starts. Your publications can be more fun—for you and for your readers. Certainly you can't write about every subject lightly, but you can write about them brightly. One thing's for sure; if you don't have fun doing your publications, your audience won't have fun reading them. If you don't think they are exciting and interesting, neither will your readers.

Much of what you write about seems to be routine, humdrum stuff. For example, suppose you're assigned to write a story about a citation the Red Cross is giving your company. Boring stuff. Not the way Susan Melanson handled it:

> It seemed a bright idea at the time.
> The North York chapter of the Canadian Red Cross Society had announced plans to give IBM Canada a citation for holding 20 years of successful blood donor clinics in Toronto.
> What better way to cover the story than by a firsthand account?
> I looked about for a likely volunteer. The other staff members winked at each other slyly when approached. "Sorry, I'm below the acceptable weight limitations," said one.
> "I've given plenty of times," said the other. "It needs a fresh approach."
> Right.
> Don't misunderstand me. Giving blood is a noble deed, and I have great respect for the countless IBMers who've done so over the years. But all those white cots, needles and rubber tubes have always made me highly nervous. Suppose I couldn't take it and collapsed from the effects?
> "Nonsense," they said.
> Mustering all the reporter bravado that flows through my veins I marched dutifully to the clinic that afternoon.
> The first step is a snap. "Would you care for a glass of orange juice? We only take sweet blood," said a chuckling woman clad in the blue Red Cross volunteer garb.

The story is interesting, entertaining and informative. The writer spices up her copy with sentences like these:

> Then she led me down the hallway to a converted board room that now looked like a scene from M.A.S.H. Unfortunately, Alan Alda was nowhere to be seen.

She ends the story this way:

> Will I ever give blood again? Let's put it this way. Clinics are held here three times a year. And when the next one rolls around, barring the onslaught of some dreaded disease, or the overwhelming desire to have a tatoo planted on my person, I'll be there.
> Why not? I lived to tell this tale.

The writer went that extra step. She did more than talk about a citation or about how and when to give blood.

You don't have to participate in an event to write a good story. Here's a paragraph from a profile by Mel Tansill about a man who has just become a bank president:

> He's the all-American boy made good. A scrawny kid who grew up on an Aberdeen farm and dreamed of becoming a banker. He enjoys his work so much that his eyes sparkle whenever he speaks about his job. In fact, if you didn't know he was 47 years old, you'd think he just got his first hit in a Little League game.

If you don't know the man, you want to get to know him. But profiles are somewhat easier to write. What do you do if you have to write the story about the company party? Here's how Jeanne Reinhart handled it:

> Cinderella's carriage turned to a pumpkin and her coachman and horses returned to their lives as mice, as the annual Triple C Club Christmas party ignored the stroke of midnight.
> Prince Charming didn't even notice Cinderella's rags through his blood-shot eyes. But then, frogs never did have excellent eyesight.
> The carriages began to arrive at the Centre Plaza Inn at 7 p.m. Friday, Dec. 4, though carriage parking was limited. Each dame and damsel was presented a long-stemmed rose as she entered the ball. Soon the hall was filled with 400 people.
> The buffet was fit for a king. . . .

The writer then tells about the menu and the guests. A different writer might have begun this story this way:

> The annual Triple C Club Christmas party was held on Dec. 4 at the Centre Plaza Inn. More than 400 attended.
> On the menu was. . . .

Even in technical writing you can be creative. Here's how a story in Beaumont Hospital's publication about an eye disease begins:

> A crisp, new dollar bill rests at the bottom of a pond. Beneath the rippling water, the straight edges of the bill appear curved. George Washington's face is lost in a greyish blur.
> For a person with an epiretinal membrane blocking his center of vision, the whole world looks as blurry and distorted as that waterlogged dollar bill.

The writer explains terms and procedures as the story moves along:

> Epiretinal membranes grow like cobwebs across the inner rim of the eyeball. They cannot be seen from the outer surface of the eye.
> The membranes are semi-transparent and, in many cases, so thin they're invisible. . . .
> Clinging to the retina, the delicate inner lining of the eyeball, the membranes interfere with the work of the macula, a central spot behind the retina that is responsible for sharpness of vision.
> To remove an epiretinal membrane, the surgeon must ever so carefully peel it off the retina with a hooked needle or retinal pick.
> According to the steady-handed Dr. Margherio, trying to peel off the membrane is like trying to pluck fingernail polish off a nylon stocking without ripping the stocking.
> If the needle should accidently tear the retina behind the membrane, the patient might lose all sight in the eye.

It's a careful, clear piece of writing. And it's done creatively. Good description is good writing. When Raytheon magazine did an article about the radar equipment it manufactures that is used on jet fighters, the story began this way:

> It looks so easy there in the brittle, clear Nevada afternoon. The F-16 jet fighter seems almost to hover like a hummingbird as it flares for touchdown. The main wheels kiss the runway with a puff of rubber, the nosewheel plants itself on the centerline, and the sleek blue-gray arrow whistles past, decelerating smoothly, the engine's roar hushed to a whisper.
>
> The pilot has just been "talked down" to one more safe arrival using a ground-controlled approach.

The writing is sensual. This awesome hunk of technology is made to be as soft and wondrous as a hummingbird.

Because Raytheon also supplies radar equipment used on the *QE2*, the magazine delighted readers with a story that began this way:

> Like that former Elizabeth, she is more than just a queen. Her passengers are surrounded by rich trappings of regal femininity. But hidden away, she has—as Elizabeth I proclaimed to her troops before the defeat of Spain's Armada—"the heart and stomach of a king." The merest hint of that deep-down power summons up an old mix of emotions: love, awe and much more besides.

The story is filled with interesting, precise information. Because of the radar equipment supplied by Raytheon, the *QE2*, which travels at 32 knots, can stop within just 1.7 miles, while a supertanker traveling at 16 knots, without that equipment, requires up to 8 miles. The ship consumes 500 tons of fuel per day, and her fuel bill for 1982 was about $30 million, nearly half the original cost of building her. When a hunk of drifting ice caused her to change course and add 18 miles to the 3,100-mile journey from Southhampton to New York, the detour cost $3,600.

The story ends this way:

> Technically, she's ahead of her time, but don't let that fool you. She is a great and glorious anachronism. Her rivals have all been scuttled by rising prices and low airfares. The world she sprang from died when we were all much younger. They did things differently then. On the *Queen*, they still do.

Throughout the story, the writer dares the reader to stop reading. Organizations ought to foster and promote more of that kind of writing. Unless they do, they are wasting time and money. No, not the readers' time. The readers will give them no time to waste.

8

grammar:
write it right

In 1414, when the Holy Roman Emperor Sigismund was criticized for his bad grammar, he replied, "I am the Roman king, and I am above grammar."

Perhaps he was, but writers are not. You should be convinced of the importance of grammar, and you should be able to apply basic grammatical principles. What columnist James J. Kilpatrick said to a meeting of Associated Press Managing Editors applies equally to you:

> We are the principal trustees of the written word. . . . As trustees we cannot allow our legacy to be frittered away. We have a high obligation, as I see it, to preserve the form and structure and beauty of our tongue, to demand a certain purity of style and syntax, to resist a Gresham's Law of language by which bad usages tend to drive out the good.

You cannot "preserve the form and structure and beauty of our tongue" without knowing the principles of accepted usage. This chapter is by no means a complete review of grammar, but it will help you avoid common errors and avoid everyday problems.

First, here are some reasons for knowing grammar:

1. Being grammatical clarifies meaning.
2. Knowing grammar provides a vocabulary for talking about language.

3. Being grammatical helps you be consistent.
4. Being grammatical is being correct.
5. Being grammatical impresses editors.

Let's look at each of these reasons:

Being grammatical clarifies meaning

Some people write just for the fun of it; others write just because they have to. But if you are like most people, you write because you have something to say. Your challenge is to transfer a message from your mind to the minds of your readers. It is the *meaning* of the message that counts. You wish to convey that meaning as easily as you can to as many readers as possible.

Knowing grammar helps you do that. If your writing is grammatical, you are using the preferred or prescribed forms in speaking and writing. Certain forms are preferred or prescribed because they enable most people to understand more easily what is written or said. If you follow grammatical principles, the meaning will be clear. Even if large numbers of people consistently break the rules, ungrammatical writing usually remains unclear.

For example, you have probably read a sentence like this one many times: "John said the boss told him he can't go." Regardless of how many people write like this, the meaning remains unclear. Who can't go, John or the boss? Or look at the common dangling modifier, in this case a dangling participle, from Gay Talese's book, *Thy Neighbor's Wife:*

> After completing high school in 1949, his sister wrote that she had arranged for him an appointment to Annapolis.

Readers have to puzzle out from the context that it was the brother, not the sister, who completed high school in 1949. Good writers say what they mean.

Now comes a problem. How do you discuss why those sentences are ambiguous without using grammatical terms? What, after all, is a participle? That brings us to the second reason for knowing grammar.

Knowing grammar provides a vocabulary for talking about language

Learning grammar is largely a matter of learning what to call words and constructions. You would wonder about a surgeon who asked the nurse for the watchamacallit. You would be surprised if a carpenter asked you to hand him the tool he needs to drive in a nail. You'd probably say, "You mean the hammer?" What if he would say, "Well, I used to know what it's called, but I keep forgetting."

Just as the carpenter needs to know his tools, writers need to know the parts of speech. You need to know how words are used and why. It's one thing to tell someone he is incorrect when he says "between you and I." It's another thing to tell him that "I" is the object of a preposition and therefore must be in the objective case. The explanation means that you know what case is, what a preposition is, and what the objective case is. There are no shortcuts. You must know the terms, and you must know the rules. If you don't, you will write one way one time and another way another time. You will commit the sin that no copy editor allows: You will be inconsistent.

Being grammatical helps you be consistent

Writers and editors spend a great deal of time deciding when to abbreviate and when to capitalize. Sometimes, the decision is arbitrary, but all agree that the copy should be consistent. An inconsistency looks like an error, and an error or the appearance of an error decreases credibility. The most simple and practical reason for being grammatical is to be consistent.

Being grammatically consistent neither stifles your creativity nor dictates uniformity. The English language is infinitely rich and flexible, and there are many ways to write a statement correctly. Grammatical principles do not restrict your freedom; rather, they free you to write clearly and precisely.

Being grammatical is being correct

There is a correct way to hold a dinner fork and many incorrect ways. There are correct ways to address various members of the clergy and many incorrect ways. Why some ways are correct and others aren't is sometimes impossible to explain. Often, the correct way is merely a matter of custom. After all, why do words mean what they mean, and why are words spelled the way they are? Critic Dwight MacDonald wrote nearly 20 years ago: "If nine-tenths of the citizens of the United States, including a recent President, were to use *inviduous*, the one-tenth who clung to *invidious* would still be right, and they would be doing a favor to the majority if they continued to maintain the point."

The same is true of grammatical principles. Most of the time we have a logical reason for insisting on correct usage. Usually, the reason is to ensure clarity. Sometimes we are grammatical because correct usage is practical, because correct usage helps us to be consistent. And sometimes we are grammatical only because we want to be correct.

For example, it is correct to use the subjective case after the verb "to be." You should say, "That was *she*." No one would misunderstand you if you were to say, "That was her," but you would be incorrect.

Being correct is often a matter of pride. When you care about how you write, you write correctly. Knowing what is correct instills pride and confidence.

You don't have to guess. For a while, you may have to apply the rules consciously. But after a while, writing correctly, like riding a bicycle, becomes second nature.

When it does, you will become fully aware that, as in all the other arts, form does not merely influence content: Form *is* content. The way you express an idea is part of that idea. You cannot separate one from the other. You have heard people say that they know what they want to say, but they just can't put their thoughts into words. A writer who has that problem should find another occupation.

Choosing the right words and putting them together in the grammatically correct way are difficult tasks of the writer. Performing these tasks well will help you sell articles or get a job as a writer.

Being grammatical impresses editors

Editors are likely to reject a story that has grammatical errors. Some editors feel that if you don't care enough to write grammatically, why should they care about reading your story? Some editors are infuriated by split infinitives. Strange behavior, perhaps. But why take the chance? You should at least be aware that you are splitting an infinitive. When your editor asks you about it, you can quote Strunk and White, who say it's all right to split an infinitive *to really emphasize* the adverb.

Even if editors aren't impressed, you should be. If writers don't care about upholding the standards of written language, who will? If writers don't demand clear expression from themselves, editors can only despair. Columnist Thomas H. Middleton wrote about the gravity of the problem:

> We are in trouble. When writers don't know the rules, their writing usually turns to mush. When writing turns to mush, thought, which feeds on writing, suffers from malnutrition and is incapable of clear development or expression.
> When that happens, the perils of this complex world become overwhelming.

Because you are a writer, you recognize that grammar helps you to talk about language, to be consistent, to be correct, to edify editors. Most important, it helps you to write clearly. As poet John Dryden said, "The chief aim of the writer is to be understood."

To help you be understood, let's review some grammar. What follows here has two purposes: To whet your appetite for grammar and to help you avoid some of the more common errors. This chapter deals with:

1. Sentences
2. Verbs and their voices, tenses and moods
3. Verbals and dangling modifiers
4. Pronouns and their cases

5. Subject and verb agreement, subject and pronoun agreement
6. Commas, semicolons, hyphens and dashes

These are the building blocks for constructing your stories. Let's begin at the foundation, the sentence.

Sentences

Sentences express complete thoughts. We expect readers to be able to grasp our meaning if we give them one complete idea at a time. A sentence has a subject and a predicate. The least a sentence can have is a noun (a person, place or thing) or a pronoun (a word that takes the place of a noun) and a verb (a word that expresses action, being or state of being). Sentences can carry much more than that, but if you want to be understood, keep most of your sentences short.

The key to the short sentence, says columnist Kilpatrick, is the period. When Kilpatrick was a young reporter, and as he says, when he was "writing interminable sentences," his city editor gave him a piece of paper with a long string of dots on it. Below the dots was this message: "These interesting objects, which apparently you have rarely encountered before, are known as periods. You will find them most helpful, and I urge you to use them."

Some writers seem averse to periods. Here is a sentence written by a young man trying to explain why he wished to enter a graduate program in journalism:

> I feel that this program best suits my needs due to the overall excellence of the training available and the flexibility built into the program, which will allow me to pursue a program planned to emphasize those areas of special importance to me while developing a generally high level of journalistic competence and determining applications for my specific capabilities.

Beginners aren't the only ones to get lost in linguistic jungles. Here is a 122-word sentence from Harrison E. Salisbury's book, *Without Fear or Favor*:

> As Sulzberger checked over his carefully packed bags, he had not the slightest premonition that publication of the Pentagon Papers story that morning was triggering a sequence of events which would lead inexorably, step by step, to the greatest disaster ever to befall an American President, a disaster so profound, so far-reaching in implication that by the time it was over basic relationships in the American power apparatus would be changed; the very system would quiver; a President would fall; the balance of the tripartite American constitutional structure would shift; and the role of the press in America, the role of the New York Times, and even the function of the press in other great nations of the world would be transformed.

Readers are not helped by a sentence like that; they are left breathless. The meaning is lost in the underbrush.

Not that every sentence should be short. If you write only short, clipped sentences, your story will not flow. You must vary the length of your sentences unless you want a staccato, machine-gun effect. You can do this by varying the types of sentences you write. Sentences can be simple, complex or compound.

a. Simple sentences.   A simple sentence consists of one independent clause. An independent clause expresses a complete thought and can stand by itself. For example:

This is a complete sentence.

b. Complex sentences.   A complex sentence has one independent and one or more dependent clauses. A dependent clause usually has little meaning when it stands by itself. For example:

Although it was raining.

As part of a complex sentence, the dependent clause makes sense:

Although it was raining, the couple strolled along slowly.

When you write a complex sentence, keep the subject close to the verb. Readers expect a subject to have a verb. They want to know what the subject is doing. Don't make them wait for the verb or wade through a dependent clause to get to it. Here's a sentence from a university publication:

> The Bert Henry Memorial Scholarship Fund, founded posthumously on the instructions of a man who believed strongly in the merits of learning although he had little formal education himself, has become one of Simon Fraser University's most prestigious graduate awards.

In this sentence, the reader can forget the subject *fund* of the sentence before getting to the verb *has become*. It is better to lead into the subject:

> Founded posthumously on the instructions of a man with little formal education, the Bert Henry Memorial Scholarship Fund has become one of Simon Fraser University's most prestigious graduate awards.

The sentence also had to be shortened. If Bert Henry left money for a scholarship fund, he obviously "believed strongly in the merits of learning." So why say it?

c. Compound sentences.   Compound sentences have two independent clauses. When you wish to show that two complete thoughts are related or are of equal value, use a compound sentence. Both of the following sentences are compound. (The subjects are underlined once and the verbs twice.)

There is abundant evidence of a plethora of potential writing talent, but publishers lack material. The system has broken down, and the breakdown is not confined to writers.

In each sentence, two complete thoughts are joined by coordinating (meaning "making equal") conjunctions or connecting words. A coordinating conjunction (*and, but, for, or, nor, yet*) in a compound sentence always has a comma preceding it. Never place a semicolon before a conjunction in a compound sentence. The semicolon in the following sentence should be a comma:

The Micronesian leaders returned home to find that their people still shared their dream of self-government; but now the prospect of falling into disfavor with the generous parent was creating insecurity and political division.

If the two complete thoughts have a close relationship, the semicolon may take the place of the conjunction. In the following sentence, the two thoughts are closely related in importance and construction.

In the village in Laos, people come and watch a person die. Consequently, I believe there is less fear of death; it is not something that is a no-no, a taboo.

Though the semicolon links two independent clauses, the comma never can do so without help from the coordinating conjunction. When the comma is used by itself, the error is called a comma splice or a run-on sentence. For example:

Phil likes to play football, he passes quite well.

This is a run-on sentence. Avoid it, even in direct quotations. Some writers try to justify the run-on in a quotation by saying that the person's words and sentences run on together. No speaker, except Victor Borge, inserts periods or commas into the conversation. That's the writer's job.

For these and every other rule of grammar, you or someone can think of an exception, especially if it's for special effect. Good writers, like other skilled craftsmen or artists, know the rules and how and when to break them for a desired effect. When criticized for ending a sentence with a preposition, Winston Churchill responded, "This is the sort of English up with which I will not put."

Although you should not separate independent clauses with commas, a series of short sentences may very well be divided by commas. Semicolons in the following series of sentences are too heavy; they break the flow of the copy:

It rained yesterday; it is raining today; and probably it will rain tomorrow.

Replace the semicolons with commas, and the sentence reads better.

Sometimes you may even want to use a fragment, a group of words resembling a dependent clause or lacking either a subject or a predicate. Because readers are accustomed to complete sentences that give them a complete idea, fragments jolt them. The interruption in the flow of the copy is useful to emphasize something. Here's Leola Floren, a writer for the Detroit News, helping us to see violinist Eugene Fodor. The two fragments are italicized.

> What makes a young man with a coffin-shaped case under his arm spring from the pack so dramatically that the Russians take notice? *Energy, mainly. Energy, drive, ambition, stamina.* Eugene Fodor is a sawed-off shotgun in a room of bottle rockets.

The fragment *Energy mainly* stops the reader. The repetition in the next fragment is in cadence: *Energy, drive, ambition, stamina.* This is good, strong writing. The writer knows what a sentence is and how to use a fragment. You should, too.

Good writers also know that the verb is the single most important word in a sentence.

Verbs and their voices, tenses and moods

Verbs express action, being or state of being. Action is more interesting than merely being. Action verbs do something, and they usually do something to something or someone else. Verbs that require objects to complete their meaning are called transitive verbs. Verbs that do not require an object to complete their meaning are intransitive verbs. Transitive verbs have a momentum of their own. They pull the reader from the subject to the object.

Depending how you use it in a sentence, the same verb can be either transitive or intransitive. Verbs that refer to the senses are such verbs. Some call them linking verbs. For example:

> He felt good. (*Felt* is an intransitive verb. *Good* is a predicate adjective, not an object.)
> He felt the softness of her lips. (*Felt* is a transitive verb, and *softness* is its direct object.)
> The quiche tasted great. (*Tasted* is an intransitive verb, and *great* is a predicate adjective, not an object.)
> He tasted the quiche. (*Tasted* is a transitive verb, and *quiche* is its direct object.)

Knowing that some verbs are intransitive will help keep you from using them incorrectly. For example, the verb "to lie," meaning "to recline," is always intransitive. Therefore, you can *lie* down, and the book can be *lying* on the table. The verb "to lay," meaning "to put or place in a horizontal position" is always a transitive verb. Therefore, the book is *lying* on the table because someone bothered to *lay* it there.

These verbs are difficult because the past tense of the verb "to lie" is "lay." It is correct to say: Yesterday, I *lay* down for an hour. The past tense of "to lay" is "laid." So it is correct to say: I *laid* the book on the table.

Note these verbs and their principal parts:

PRESENT TENSE	PAST TENSE	PAST PARTICIPLE
lie (to tell a falsehood) (intransitive)	lied	lied
lie (to recline) (intransitive)	lay	lain
lay (to put or place in a horizontal position) (transitive)	laid	laid
sit (to be seated) (intransitive)	sat	sat
set (to place) (transitive)	set	set
rise (to get up from a lying, sitting or kneeling position) (intransitive)	rose	risen
raise (to move to a higher position) (transitive)	raised	raised

Another verb that is always intransitive is "to be." It is sometimes called a linking verb or the copulative and never takes an object. For this reason, the more often you avoid the verb "to be," the more movement and action your writing will have. Transitive verbs pull the reader to the object. Instead of saying, "It was raining hard," pick an action verb: "The rain *pummeled* the windshield." The verb, "pummeled," makes the reader ask, "Pummeled what?" Study the transitive verbs in this news story:

Two years after Proposition 13 *rocked* California, Massachusetts *registered* a powerful aftershock: Last month voters overwhelmingly *approved* a measure that *will slash* property taxes by an average 41 percent and *drain* $1.3 billion from local coffers next year.

The lead refers, of course, to California's propensity for earthquakes. The lead is more powerful than if the writer had said:

Proposition 13 *has been* a law for two years in California, and now Massachusetts *is* in the same situation.

Another reason to avoid the verb "to be" is that it is wordy, as in these verb-adjective combinations that have no action:

He *is hopeful* of an easy win.

He *is needful* of more practice.

Make them:

He *hopes* to win easily.
He *needs* more practice.

Also, avoid the verb "to be" with the expletive (words such as *it, here* and *there* when they have no special meaning of their own). Instead of:

It is his wish to remain here for an hour.

Make it:

He wishes to remain here for an hour.

Especially avoid the expletive with a verb in the passive voice:

It was estimated by police that the accident occurred about midnight.

The sentence is punchier and shorter this way:

Police estimated that the accident occurred about midnight.

Even without the expletive, you should usually avoid the passive voice.

a. The voices of verbs.   Verbs can be in the active or the passive voice. A verb is in the active voice if the subject of the sentence is doing the acting:

In the third inning, George Brett *drove* the ball over the centerfield wall.

Drove is in the active voice. *Brett,* the subject of the sentence, did the driving. When a verb is in the passive voice, the subject of the sentence is being acted upon rather than doing the acting:

In the third inning, the ball *was driven* over the wall by George Brett.

In this sentence, *ball,* the subject of the sentence, was acted upon. The ball *was driven.* The verb is in the passive voice. Here's how to recognize it:
    First, the form of the verb "to be" is always present: "*was* driven."
    Second, the past participle is always present: "was *driven.*"
    Third, the preposition "by" is always there or understood: "*by* George Brett."
    That's how to recognize the passive voice. Here's why you should avoid using it:

First, it's wordy. The added word "to be" is always there, and the preposition "by" is usually there.

Second, the past participle makes the verb sound past, even when the present is intended. "It is suggested by experts" sounds past. "Experts suggest" sounds present, and it is.

Third, readers usually want to know who or what is doing the acting. Sometimes, the doer of the action does not want to take responsibility, or the writer does not wish to assign responsibility. Look at this sentence:

> Politicians, government writers, corporation writers and academicians often *are accused* of writing in the passive voice in order to avoid clearly assigning responsibility.

The verb, *are accused*, is in the passive voice, and the preposition "by" is missing. As a result, the reader never learns who did the accusing. The writer neither takes the responsibility for the statement nor assigns it to someone else.

Fourth, the passive voice isn't as dynamic as the active. These two sentences illustrate the difference:

> With three seconds to go, the winning field goal *was kicked* by Efren Herrera.
> With three seconds to go, Efren Herrera *kicked* the winning field goal.

The second sentence has action. The doer is doing something. The sentence has more punch.

In spite of all the reasons for using the active voice, the passive should not be avoided altogether. Sometimes the subject being acted upon is more important than the actor, and therefore should come first in the sentence. For example:

> Southern Italy *was devastated* today by a massive earthquake.

Earthquakes are common; where this one happened is what's important. The active voice de-emphasizes the location:

> A massive earthquake today *devastated* southern Italy.

When you do not know the doer of the action, the passive voice is useful.

> The car *was stolen* sometime between midnight and 1 a.m.

You would hardly want to write:

> Some thief stole the car sometime between midnight and 1 a.m.

You may even wish to use the passive voice for a change of pace or variation in your writing. But use it sparingly.

Don't use the present tense sparingly.

b. The tenses of verbs.   Reporters writing about past events usually put the verbs in the past tense. But many, if not most, of the features and profiles you write would be improved if you used the present tense. The present tense indicates that what happened or what was said continues into the present. If you write, " 'I liked my job,' he said," it sounds as if he no longer likes it. If you write, " 'I like my job,' he says," you are saying that he still does. This is illustrated by this paragraph from Ambassador magazine:

> Without a "common ground" of rules that *are understood* and *obeyed*, people *can* no longer use language to communicate, (Edwin) Newman *says*. When the language *fills* with gas, people can no longer examine what they *are being told*, and they *run* the risk of *being deceived*. Pompous language *is* simply boring; Newman *says* that most people will never take an interest in politics until politicians *begin* to speak plainer.

You can be sure from this paragraph and the use of the present tense that Edwin Newman continues his battle against the abusers of language. The verbs in the present tense indicate that what Newman said at the time of the interview he would say today.

The present tense can be used then to indicate what is happening now and what always, repeatedly or habitually occurs:

> She *rides* the bus every morning.
> They often *walk* to school.

You can also use the present to indicate future time:

> The plane *leaves* in one hour.
> Reagan *flies* to California on Thursday.

The historical present refers to events completed in the past. It is more often used in headlines, but it is useful also in many types of stories. The headline, "Reagan *leaves* for California," means, of course, that Reagan has already left. In a story, the historical present describes more vividly what took place in past time:

> It *is* 6:30 a.m. on a spring Monday morning. Bill Middleton *wakes* up at his home in the Roland Park section of Baltimore. He *eats* a toasted muffin, *drinks* a cup of grapefruit juice, and then *takes* his English bulldog, Darwin, for a walk around the neighborhood. He has done the same thing each morning for the past seven years. Only one thing is different. Now he *is* the president of Equitable Trust Company.

The story continues to follow the new bank president for a day. The historical present works here, and you should try to use it as often as you can. Of course, the past tense has its place, especially in the straight news story. You would ordinarily use the past tense in a story telling of a past event like a meeting, press conference, accident, and such.

The past tense indicates that the action is completed. The past tense of most verbs is formed by adding "ed" to the stem of the verb. The past participle is formed the same way. Such verbs are called "regular." "Irregular" verbs have different forms for the past tense and the past participle. For example, the past tense of "go" is "went," and the past participle is "gone."

The past participle, preceded by a form of a helping verb ("to be" or "to have"), is used to form the perfect tenses. You should pay special attention to the present perfect tense because it denotes an action that continues into the present. The difference between the past and present perfect tenses is illustrated in these two sentences:

Sarah Jacobsen *lived* in Crown Point for more than one year. (past tense)
Sarah Jacobsen *has lived* in Crown Point for more than one year. (present perfect tense)

In the first sentence, the verb indicates completed action: Sarah no longer lives there. The second sentence clearly means that Sarah continues to live there.

The present perfect tense can also indicate completed action at the present:

The House *has voted* overwhelmingly to block a shipment of uranium fuel to India.

Notice that the verb here indicates more immediacy than the simple past:

The House *voted* overwhelmingly to block a shipment of uranium fuel to India.

Many times the immediacy of the present perfect is preferable to the past. Broadcast writers, for example, prefer the present and the present perfect tense. They want their news to have the sound of immediacy and continuation. Print journalists can capitalize on the same strengths.

The progressive form of the verb also helps denote immediacy. The progressive indicates that the action is continuing at the time noted. You form the progressive by placing some form of the verb "to be" before the present participle. The present participle is formed by adding "ing" to the stem of the verb. Note these verbs in the past progressive:

Interest rates *were approaching* the record levels set last spring, inflation was again on the boil and the economy *was teetering* on the brink of another slump—the second scoop in a "double dip" that Reagan's men *were coming* to accept as inevitable.

Even though all of these events occurred in the past, the use of the progressive conveys a sense of action and immediacy. Use it when your story permits it.

You need to know and use all of the tenses, but remember especially the present and the present perfect, as well as all of the forms of the progressive.

c. The moods of verbs.   In addition to voices and tenses, verbs have moods or modes. The mood of the verb is determined by the attitude the speaker or writer has toward the sentence. When you make a simple statement of fact or ask a question, you use the indicative mood. For example:

She *is* my friend.

When you make a request or a command, you use the imperative mood:

Always *write* grammatically.

When you express a doubt, a wish, or a condition contrary to fact, you use the subjunctive mood. The subjunctive is less well understood and needs more attention than the other moods. First, let's conjugate the verb "to be" in the present and past tense of the subjunctive mood:

(present tense)	I be	we be
	you be	you be
	he (she, it) be	they be
(past tense)	I were	we were
	you were	you were
	he (she, it) were	they were

The present subjunctive is used when you wish to express a doubt, a wish or something that's a possibility.

If he *be* guilty, he should be punished.

If you wish to express a condition contrary to fact, you must use the past subjunctive:

If I *were* you, I would learn the subjunctive.

In the second case, I am not you, and I never can be you. It is a condition contrary to fact. However, not every "if" is followed by a verb in the subjunctive. Consider the difference between these two statements:

If I *was* there, I don't remember.
If I *were* there, I would be fishing.

In the first sentence, the verb is in the past tense, indicative mood. The speaker is indicating that he believes he was not there. The verb in the second sentence is in the past tense, subjunctive mood. The speaker knows that he is not there. He is expressing a condition contrary to fact.

As a writer, you need to know that a speaker is saying something quite different when he uses the subjunctive rather than the indicative. You need to study other uses of the subjunctive. Learning it, like learning any grammar, will give you the "pleasure and amusement and satisfaction" of using the language well, as Newman says. Even if no one else appreciates your correct usage, you will.

Verbals and dangling modifiers. Verbals are forms of the verb that are used as other parts of speech. The verbals are the participle, the gerund and the infinitive.

We have discussed how the present and past participles are formed and how they are used in the progressive and perfect tenses:

> She is *going* home. (present participle)
> She has *gone* home. (past participle)

We also use participles as verbal adjectives; that is, participles have some of the properties of a verb and some of the properties of an adjective. They can modify a noun (the *sleeping* child, the *required* amount), or they can take an object (the man *wearing* the hat).

When you begin a sentence with a participial phrase, be sure that the understood subject of the participle is the same as the subject of the main clause. If it isn't, you have a dangling participle:

PARTICIPIAL PHRASE

Sitting in the driver's seat, the car was obviously too small for her.

The participial phrase modifies *car*, but it should modify the person in the driver's seat. The sentence should be rewritten this way:

Sitting in the driver's seat, she became aware that the car was too small for her.

The principle is the same when you use the past participle:

Denied a raise or a promotion, the job became tedious and boring.

Again, the job was not denied a raise or a promotion. The sentence must be rewritten:

Denied a raise or a promotion, he found the job tedious and boring.

Now let's look at the gerund, which is a verbal noun. The gerund is formed in the same way as the present participle and is sometimes called a participial noun. The gerund may take an object (she likes *playing* chess), and it may be modified by an adjective or by an adverb (tiresome *droning; swimming* vigorously). As you do with a participial phrase, be careful when you begin a sentence with a gerund phrase. Make sure the understood subject of the gerund is the same as that of the main clause. Here's an example of a dangling gerund phrase:

GERUND PHRASE

After *swimming* in the cold water, the warm sand felt good on our toes.

Swimming is a gerund, the object of the preposition *after*. But the warm sand didn't swim. Rewrite it:

After swimming in the cold water, we enjoyed the warm sand on our toes.

The infinitive is also a verbal noun. It is formed by placing the preposition "to" before the stem of the verb, as in "to jog." Because the infinitive is one grammatical unit, ordinarily you should not place an adverb between "to" and the verb, "to easily do." Don't dangle an infinitive phrase either:

INFINITIVE PHRASE

To break a record, the race must be run in three minutes.

The race cannot break a record. Rewrite it:

To break a record, you must run the race in three minutes.

Don't dangle your thoughts before the reader. Place them firmly in their proper places. Good writers pay attention to verbs and verbals. They also use pronouns correctly.

Pronouns and their cases

To use the pronoun correctly, you must understand the grammatical cases. Cases indicate the relationship of nouns and pronouns to other words in a sentence. Only nouns and pronouns have cases. In English, nouns change their form only in the possessive case. Pronouns change their form for each case. You choose the form of the pronoun by how you use it in a sentence.

For all practical purposes, English has only three cases: the subjective (or nominative), objective and possessive. Let's look at the declensions (the inflections according to case) of the pronouns:

PERSONAL PRONOUNS			CASES			
Gender	Number	Person	Subjective	Objective	Possessive Short form	Long form
masculine feminine neuter	singular	1st 2nd 3rd	I you he she it	me you him her it	my your his her its	mine yours his hers its
	plural	1st 2nd 3rd	we you they	us you them	our your their	ours yours theirs

RELATIVE AND INTERROGATIVE PRONOUNS				
singular & plural	who	whom	whose	whose

Now let's look at how and when they are used.

a. The subjective case. Use the subjective case when the pronoun is the subject of the sentence.

He and *I* are going.

You would not say:

Me and *him* are going.

You also use the subjective case after the verb "to be." For example:

It is *I.*
This is *she.*
These are *they.*

Grammarians call this construction (a noun or a pronoun following the verb "to be") the predicate nominative. In ordinary conversation, you will often hear, "It's me," or, "That's us." But when you are writing, ordinarily you should be grammatically correct.

b. The objective case. The objective case is used in the following instances:
First, the pronoun is in the objective case when it is the direct object of a verb. Here are some examples:

Wrong: I hit *he*.
Right: I hit *him*.
Wrong: She dislikes *he* and *I*.
Right: She dislikes *him* and *me*.
Wrong: They took my husband and *I* to dinner.
Right: They took my husband and *me* to dinner.

Second, use the objective case when the pronoun is the indirect object of a verb. The indirect object either has the preposition "to" in front of it or "to" is understood. For example:

Throw the ball to *me*.
Throw *me* the ball.

In both examples, *me* is in the objective case because it is the indirect object. The word *ball* is the direct object. You would not write:

He spoke to *I* about it.

Or:

He spoke to *he* and *I* about it.

Neither should you write:

He spoke to my wife and *I* about it.

Instead, be correct:

He spoke to my wife and *me* about it.

Third, use the objective case when the pronoun is the object of a preposition. A preposition shows the relation between its object and some other word or part of a sentence. For example:

He walked behind *her*.

Behind is a preposition, and *her* is the object in the objective case. Again, note the compound:

Just between *you* and *me*, this is an important example.

Archie Bunker always says "between you and me," but more sophisticated folks are prone to say, "between you and I." Archie is correct.

In an interview with Harry Stein in Esquire magazine, playwright Tennessee Williams is quoted as saying: "The principal difference between he and I is stamina." Tennessee Williams incorrectly used the subjective case instead of the objective ("him and me").

Fourth, use the objective case when the pronoun is the subject of an infinitive:

They begged *me* (not *I*) to go.

This is true also in the compound:

They begged *John* and *me* to go.

John and *me* are subjects of the infinitive.

Fifth, use the objective case as the subject and the object of the infinitive "to be":

She thought *him* to be *me*.

Both the subject and the object of the infinitive are in the objective case, even when that infinitive is "to be."

Similarly, when gerunds have objects, the objects must be in the objective case.

Helping Phyllis and *me* was most kind of you.

c. The possessive case. The possessive case is used to show possession. You form the possessive case of most nouns by adding an apostrophe and an "s" to the noun, as in "Bill's." Or you may show possession by using the preposition "of" in front of the noun:

This is the house *of* John.

Or you may use the preposition "of" and the noun in the possessive case:

He is a friend *of John's.*

Unlike the noun, the pronoun in the possessive case never takes an apostrophe. The possessive case of the pronouns all have their own form:

This is *my* house. This is *mine.*
This is *your* house. This is *yours.*
This is *his* house. This is *his.*
This is *her* house. This is *hers.*
This is *their* house. This is *theirs.*

This is *its* place.

Note especially the possessive case of the pronoun "it." When you write "it's," you are writing the contraction for "it is." You never write "its'."

You may also form the possessive of the pronoun by using the preposition "of" along with the pronoun in the possessive case. For example:

This is one *of hers*.

Pay special attention to the pronoun "who." It is either an interrogative pronoun or a relative pronoun. Interrogative pronouns (*who, whom, whose, which and what*) introduce questions. Relative pronouns (*who, whom, whose, which and that*) connect a dependent clause to an antecedent in another clause. Look at these uses:

Who is going? (Interrogative pronoun)
Did you say *who* is going? (Relative pronoun)
I don't know *who* it is. (Relative pronoun)

In all the examples, *who* is in the subjective case. In the second example, *who is going* is the direct object of the verb *say*, but *who* is the subject of *is going*.

In the third example, the clause is inverted. *Who* is the predicate nominative: *it is who*.

The same is true in this example:

Who did you say was going?

Who is the subject of *was going*, although *who was going* is the object of *say*. Another difficult case:

The Cardinals, *who* they said wouldn't come close to winning, lost by one point.

In this example, *who* is the subject of *wouldn't come close to winning*.
And one more:

To the question of *who* was going, he had no reply.

Even though *who* looks like the object of a preposition, it must be in the subjective case because it is the subject of *was going*.

The objective case of "who" is "whom." In the sentence, "Whom did he choose?," *whom* is the direct object of the verb *choose*. The same is true in this sentence:

He didn't say *whom* he would choose.

Note also the use of "whom" as the object of a preposition: To *whom* are you speaking?

In conversation you might say, *"Who* are you speaking to?" But you are not grammatically correct.

The possessive case of "who" is "whose" and not "who's," which is a contraction of "who is." Hence:

Whose is this?
Bill, *who's* (*who is*) a natural leader, handled it well.

Before we leave the pronoun, let's look at the intensive and reflexive forms. They have the same forms (*myself, yourself, yourselves, himself, herself, itself, ourselves, themselves*) but are used differently. The intensive is used to add emphasis:

I *myself* don't feel that way.

The reflexive pronoun refers an action to the subject of the sentence:

I hurt *myself.*

The intensive and reflexive pronouns are seldom used wrong in these situations, but often they are used incorrectly as the subject of a sentence:

The chancellor and *myself* agree.

The correct use, of course, is: The chancellor and *I* agree.

As in the case of the verb, this treatment of the pronoun in no way exhausts its correct and incorrect uses. But if you master this material, you will avoid the most common errors. You may wish to explore the subject further.

Subject and verb agreement; subject and pronoun agreement

Let's look first at subjects and their verbs.

Plural subjects *require* a plural verb.
A singular subject *requires* a singular verb.

In the following sentence, the verb is singular when it should be plural:

Attempts by the Synanon Foundation to improve its public image *was* thwarted here when officials refused to appear before members of the press.

When a sentence has more than one subject (a compound subject), the verb must be plural:

Mary and I *are studying* grammar.

Sometimes when the compound subject is more complicated, writers forget to use the plural verb:

One passenger, who is on her way to Japan, and another, who is headed for Hong Kong, *are* without boarding passes.

Are is correct because there are two passengers. You must be careful when a prepositional phrase follows the subject. If the subject of the sentence is singular, it takes a singular verb, even when it is followed by a plural object of a preposition:

One of the passengers *is* a Korean.

Despite the plural object of the preposition, *passengers*, the verb is determined by the singular subject *one*. Look at the verb in this relative clause:

One of the passengers *who are* en route to Japan is Korean.

In this sentence, *who* refers to *the passengers*. It is therefore plural and needs a plural verb.

Another vexing problem you often face is determining whether a collective noun should have a singular or a plural verb. Grammarians have a simple rule, but unfortunately, it is not easy to apply: If you consider the people represented by the collective noun as individuals, you need a plural verb. Both of these usages could be correct:

The faculty (as a group) *is* meeting.
The faculty (as individuals) *are* incompetent.

Generally, however, you will use the singular verb because you will consider the collective noun as a unit. Also, common usage makes the singular verb sound better to our ears: The group *is* waiting. Because the noun appears to be singular, the verb sounds better in the singular. In "The board *have* reached a decision," the plural verb jars the ear. If you wish to emphasize strongly that you are referring to the individuals in the collective noun, use the plural verb.

Indefinite pronouns such as *each, every, none, everybody, everyone, anybody, nobody, neither,* and *either* are all singular and take a singular verb. These words present a problem with the pronoun. If the verb is singular, then the pronoun is singular. Do not write:

The company *is* dividing *their* stock.
Everyone *is* doing *their* thing.

In the first example, the company is an "it" and needs the pronoun "its." In the second example, you meet the problem of sexist language face-to-face. Grammarians used to say that when a singular pronoun refers to a noun with no gender, the pronoun is to be masculine. Here's how an 1868 grammar states it:

> The English language being destitute of a pronoun of the third person singular and common gender, usage has sanctioned the employment of the masculine form, he, his, him, for the purpose.

Hence:

> Everyone *is* doing *his* thing.
> A writer *deserves his* pay.

It is this second example that is the most disturbing. Why are most professions and occupations masculine? Is it true that because of our use of the masculine pronoun in these instances young women exclude themselves from these professions and occupations? If this is even a possibility, should we not do something about our language?

Yet, no writer seriously wishes to use "his/her" or "her/his" every time this comes up. If you do this, the pronouns will distract dreadfully from the flow and meaning of the sentences:

> A writer should do *his/her* homework before going out on *his/her* interview. *She/he* should check Who's Who for biographical background so that *he/she* will know the interviewee better.

Others think the solution is to alternate the use of "he" and "she." They would have us do it this way:

> A writer should do *her* homework before going on *his* interview. *She* should check Who's Who for biographical background so that *he* will know the interviewee better.

That solution is patently absurd. It hopelessly confuses the reader. The only sensible solution most of the time is to use the plural:

> Writers should do *their* homework before going out on *their* interviews. *They* should check Who's Who for biographical background so that *they* will know the interviewee better.

Here as elsewhere, the important thing is that you at least are grammatical and consistent. Solutions to problems of sexist language should be sought with that in mind. You must also be consistent in your punctuation.

Commas, semicolons, hyphens
and dashes

Like the precise choice of words, correct punctuation helps the reader grasp the meaning of a sentence. Careful writers do not regard punctuation lightly or consider it peripheral to the writing process. Some rules of punctuation are arbitrary. Unlike grammar rules, some punctuation rules are dependent upon the medium. Book and magazine punctuation is usually more formal than punctuation in newspapers. Thus, where formal rules of punctuation require a comma after items in a series, newspapers dispense with the last one:

Commas, semicolons, hyphens and dashes are often misused.

Newspaper style of punctuation, as suggested by the AP and UPI stylebooks, is austere. Punctuation marks are left out unless clarity demands them. You would do well to adopt these stylebooks because your style would then conform to most newspapers and to a large number of magazines and newsletters. *Words into Type* is another marvelously complete volume of style rules.

Rules of punctuation often go hand in hand with grammatical rules. Knowledge of grammar will enable you to punctuate correctly and with confidence.

a. The comma.   Particularly vexing is the comma. Some say commas have no rules, but they are wrong.

Commas generally separate or mark the boundaries of certain structures. We also tend to pause at the boundaries of these structures. In most instances, if a comma causes readers to pause and keeps them from having to reread the sentence, by all means use one. Introductory clauses almost always require a comma. Short introductory phrases ordinarily do not.

Wrong: A child without a real home Charles had nowhere to turn.
Correct: A child without a real home, Charles had nowhere to turn.
Wrong: After the meal was served he stood up to leave.
Correct: After the meal was served, he stood up to leave.

When the dependent clause follows the independent clause, usually a comma is not required: *He stood up to leave after the meal was served.*

A comma rule more easily applied deals with apposition. A word, phrase or clause is said to be in apposition when what it says merely adds to the meaning of the sentence and is not essential to the meaning:

The student, *who is not very bright,* missed the point entirely.

The clause *who is not very bright* is non-essential information. In grammatical terms, it is non-restrictive. The test is whether the clause changes the meaning of the sentence. Look at this sentence:

The boy who is wearing the green shirt should be watched.

The clause *who is wearing a green shirt* is essential because it designates which boy should be watched. Because the clause is essential for the identification of the boy, it is restrictive. By not using commas you make clear the meaning of the sentence. Here's another example:

Tom's daughter Mary is 16, and his son, Tom, is 9.

This sentence indicates that Tom has more than one daughter, but only one son. Because *Mary* is essential to know which daughter, no commas are used. On the other hand, *Tom* is set off by commas because it is non-essential information.

The relative pronoun "which" is most often used in an appositional clause. "Which" indicates that the clause is merely additional information.

The house, *which* badly needs repairs, is for sale.

Notice how the meaning of the sentence changes when you use the word "that."

The house *that* badly needs repairs is for sale.

Here the "that" clause is essential to the identification of the house. Always use "that" instead of "which" when you wish to write an essential, restrictive clause. A "that" clause never needs a comma before or after it; a "which" clause always does.

We must become which-hunters, Strunk and White say. Too often, "which" is used when writers mean "that." An additional reason for knowing the difference is to help you know when to use commas.

One more word about apposition. One comma of apposition always demands another one, unless the sentence ends with the apposition. Note the following:

The third house, which has green shutters is George's.

The sentence needs a comma after *shutters*. Another example:

The third house that has green shutters, is George's.

This sentence should not have a comma after *shutters*. Also note the difference between the meanings of the sentences. In the sentence with "which," you would simply count the houses to find George's. In the "that" sentence, you would have to count the houses with green shutters to find George's. The meaning of the two sentences is quite different and important—if you want to find George's house. Correct usage and correct punctuation make the difference.

Another comma rule deals with coordinate adjectives. Coordinate adjectives are adjectives of equal rank. In the following example, both adjectives modify the noun equally:

The *tall, narrow* skyscraper reached for the sun.

If adjectives are coordinate, they can be interchanged without changing the meaning.

The *narrow, tall* skyscraper reached for the sun.

Also, if they are coordinate, you can use the conjunction "and" between them.

The tall *and* narrow skyscraper reached for the sun.

Coordinate adjectives always need a comma between them. Not all adjectives do:

The *tired old* man needed a drink.

You would not write:

The *old, tired* man needed a drink.

The adjective *old* outweighs the adjective *tired*. *Old* needs to go with man. The adjectives are not coordinate. They should not have a comma between them.

As noted earlier, remember to put a comma before a coordinating conjunction in a compound sentence.

b. The semicolon.   For all practical purposes, the semicolon has only two purposes. First, it breaks up major divisions in a series that already has commas.

The list included: Phil Able, 29, of 145 E. Elm St.; Jeremy Wilks, 31, of 432 W. Ash; and Jim Blaney, 19, of 371 N. Main.

The second use of the semicolon shows a close relationship between the two independent clauses of a compound sentence. As was noted earlier, the semicolon in this instance takes the place of the coordinating conjunction:

Talese writes that "Bullaro would sometimes peddle alone for fifteen miles." But Bullaro is not selling something; he is a man pedaling a bicycle.

The last two sentences are closely connected; hence, the semicolon.

c. The hyphen. When you have a doubt about whether an individual word has a hyphen, you have little choice but to look it up in a good dictionary or in your stylebook. The trend today is to remove the hyphen whenever possible. Hence, you write "nonapplicable," rather than "non-applicable."

Middle-class families seem hardest hit by the recession.

Middle does not modify *families. Class* does not describe *families* adequately. The families are *middle-class. Middle-class* is a compound modifier.
Notice the non-use and the use of the hyphen in the following:

She was *8 years old. (8 years old* stands on its own; *8 years* modifies *old,* and *old* is a predicate adjective)
She acted like an *8-year-old* child. (*8-year-old* modifies "child"; it is a compound modifier)
She acted like an *8-year-old.* (*child* is understood; again, *8-year-old* is a compound modifier)

Knowing grammar also will help you know when not to hyphenate. For example, because you know that an adverb can never modify a noun, you know that you should not hyphenate an adverb. Note this incorrect example:

His *badly-damaged* car was near the house.

Badly does not and cannot modify the noun *car. Badly* modifies the past participle *damaged.* Hence, *badly damaged* cannot be a compound modifier and should not be hyphenated. The same is true of all adverbs. Nevertheless, to simplify and to be consistent, both AP and UPI hyphenate all adverbs except those ending in "ly" and the adverb "very."
One more about word about hyphens. Some writers go berserk with them:

The *crucifix-emblazoned* jumbo jet landed on the tarmac. The *church-enlisted* marshals kept the crowds away. Invoking the names of *centuries-old* saints, the Pope prayed for *schism-split* churches and the *folk-singing, fiddle-playing* outdoor Mass.

Perhaps the Pope should have prayed for hyphen-mad writers. And while he was at it, he should have prayed for writers who are too *dash-oriented* (avoid using any words hyphenated with "-oriented" or "-wise").

d. The dash.   Don't be a dasher. A dash should be used for emphasis or for a dramatic break in the sentence. Some grammarians allow the dash to substitute for simple apposition or for parenthetical expressions. Apposition takes commas, and parenthetical expressions need parentheses. Like the exclamation point, use the dash sparingly. If you emphasize everything, nothing is emphasized. On the other hand, you can use the dash effectively:

If you're thinking this is unimportant—forget it!

Most of all, don't use the dash just because you have written yourself into a hole and can't get out. Too many times we tack on afterthoughts by using a dash, and end up with long, incoherent sentences:

The product was of little use to the company, although some expressed satisfaction—even if they didn't do so aloud.

The sentence would be better:

The product was of little use to the company, although some tacitly expressed satisfaction.

Don't underplay the importance of punctuation. Precision here is as important as the precise choice of words and the correct use of grammar. All will make your meaning clearer to readers, and that's what good writing is all about.

Grammar and punctuation rules are not easy to learn, but nothing worthwhile is. You will need to come back to this chapter and to study other grammar books. You may come to feel as University of Missouri student Diana Dawson did:

A few months ago, the mechanics of grammar were nitpicking; today, they are the tools of a struggling writer.

9

words
and what they do
to people

By now, you know good writing when you see it. You know how to achieve it. But do you know why it's good? Many writers don't really know why one verb is preferable to another, why one description is clearer than another, why one sentence communicates more effectively than another. You'll be a better writer if you do know.

This chapter will help. It will help by showing you what words do to people and vice versa. Research has shown that the nature of language itself dictates what effective writing is. To find out why some uses of language work better, communicate better, than others, you need to look more closely than most writers do at the words that are a writer's tools.

General semantics does that. By studying its principles, you can develop a deeper appreciation of language and its effects. You can come to understand something of the theory that underlies the practice of good writing. If, in addition to knowing what works, you know why it works, you can choose and use your words more carefully.

This chapter won't make you an expert in general semantics, but it will introduce you to principles you may find helpful. You may be surprised to discover that such a seemingly esoteric subject has intensely practical applications.

General semantics is the study of how language affects human behavior. We are using the phrase general semantics for a purpose. Semantics, the study of words and what they mean, is related to linguistics. It studies how words come to be what they are and how they came to mean what they mean to various people at various times.

General semantics is neither the study of words nor the study of meaning. It does not concern itself with the *correct* meanings of words. In one sense, it teaches you just the opposite. General semantics demonstrates that words have many meanings, or more precisely, that people have or bring many meanings to words.

This is not to say that words are unimportant. On the contrary, words are so important that we must constantly evaluate what they do to us. Spoken and written words have a physical reality, and they have a *physico*logical effect on us, not just a *psycho*logical effect. Words affect our nervous systems physically. They can trigger joy, fear, anger, even violence.

Because words are so important, Alfred Korzybski, the founder of general semantics, hoped to train people to use and to evaluate language more effectively. Effective communication, he wrote, is necessary for human cooperation, human survival and human sanity. Korzybski taught not only to use words carefully but also to avoid reacting to them automatically. He urged us to delay our reaction to words. He called for a calm, mature, reflective approach to language.

His advice is particularly valuable to the reporter, and every writer must first be a reporter. We must pay attention to what people say, yes, but we must go beyond that. We must ask, what did the person mean by those words? Korzybski wanted us to realize that *how* people use words is often as important to communication as *what* words they use.

What he was asking for was a scientific approach to the sane use of language. Toward this end, he published *Science and Sanity* in 1933. It is the scientific approach to language outlined in this book that is so important to the writer.

THE WRITER AS SCIENTIST

The methods of science are useful long before you choose the words you are going to write. First, look at the world the way the scientist does. The scientist recognizes that everything is in the process of change. The world of moving molecules and atoms only confirms what the Greek philosopher Heraclitus said long ago: You never step into the same river twice.

Scientists hold that no two things are the same, that no one thing is ever the same twice, that everything is in a state of flux. As an observer gathering information, you would do well to recognize the same principle.

Don't be one of those who say that if you've seen one, you've seen them all. Scientists do not begin by looking for what is the same in things; they look for differences. Only when they can find no differences do they categorize, classify or make general laws. To an untrained or inobservant person, things look the same when they are actually different. Sometimes, of course, when things look different, you should pay attention to their similarities.

Look for similarity among differences and for the differences among things that look the same. Look for the new, for the different, for what others do not see, because what is new and different is also usually interesting.

The semanticist Wendell Johnson writes that the scientist is a "master of discrimination." Scientists are adaptable; they test everything, expect things to change; they are expert at changing their minds. You must imitate their approach. You must dissect and assemble; you must analyze with synthesis. You must be able to set aside what is insignificant and get to the core of things. Ernest Hemingway once said that the most essential gift for a good writer is a built-in, shock-proof crap detector.

If you want your writing to be interesting, you must be a careful, flexible, interested observer. The scientist, writes Johnson, "has a nose for the new, the exceptional, the fine shades of variation in the world about him and in himself and his social relationships." He could have written the same about the writer. The scientist is skeptical, cautious, not easily taken in, distrustful. The scientist looks twice. "The children of science," Johnson writes, "are from Missouri."

Missourians say, "Show me." You should do that, first, in your observation and preparation, and then in your writing. Perhaps the best advice ever given to writers is this simple sentence: "Don't tell me—show me!" But you cannot show your readers unless you have the information, unless you have observed, unless you have asked the right questions.

The scientific method begins by asking clear and answerable questions. That means that scientists must have some idea of where they are going, some hypothesis, some definite thing they are looking for. They continually refine their questions because they cannot find clear answers to vague, general questions.

Before you write, you must have a clear, answerable question. If you do not, your story will have no focus. Just as clear questions direct the scientists' observations, so will they direct yours. Scientists observe calmly and without prejudice. Their observations must be reported as accurately and objectively as possible so as to answer the original questions. Any preconceptions or assumptions must be revised in light of new observations.

Another semanticist, Kenneth Johnson, says the writer must imitate the anthropologist. You must stand apart, stand back, observe, question and record.

The process, of course, does not stop. The scientific method is continuous. The reporting and the revising go on and on. Reporters, like scientists, are forever changing their minds.

All that is demanded is that you do so with clarity. In the scientific method, clarity is paramount because without clarity there is no validity. Clarity comes by means of words. As Korzybski wrote, all science is ultimately verbal.

General semantics, then, urges a scientific approach, first of all, to the universe, to all of life. This approach will help you to gather information for your stories. General semantics also teaches a scientific approach to language, to the words you use to describe that universe.

THE BASIC PRINCIPLES
OF GENERAL SEMANTICS

Scientists see everything as changing. We must look at words the same way. Korzybski says we must never think that words can be identified with what they represent. He states three versions of one principle:

1. The symbol is not the thing symbolized.
2. The map is not the territory.
3. The word is not the thing.

A symbol is something that represents something else. It has an existence and an identity of its own, but its purpose is to signify something other. A country's flag, for example, reminds people of their country and of all that their country stands for. Treating the flag with respect is a sign of one's respect for his or her country. Many have tried to make it a crime to burn the flag, so closely is the symbol tied to the thing symbolized.

For many during the 1960s, the peace sign was a warm, human symbol of an international movement for peace. That same sign for many others was a symbol of an unpatriotic, un-American acceptance of defeat in the Vietnam War, perhaps even representing a leaning toward communism.

Some signs, such as the Nazi swastika or the cross, are so closely identified with what they symbolize that just displaying them can cause strong emotional reaction. West Germany has had a law for many years banning the display of the swastika. The American Jewish Congress has been urging U.S. toy makers to halt production and sale of war toys bearing Nazi insignia. Interestingly, the leader of one motorcycle gang said members wore swastikas to show their contempt for fascism. The same symbol can mean different things to different people. Obviously, then, the symbol is not the thing symbolized.

You must be constantly aware that, as semanticist S.I. Hayakawa says, "The symbolic process permeates human life at the most primitive and the most civilized levels alike." You must be conscious of symbols and not be misled by them. What people wear often symbolize their occupation or affiliation. But because a young lady on a college campus wears Greek letters on the seat of her pants does not necessarily mean that she is going to college or that she is member of that sorority.

Symbols, like everything else, mean different things at different times. Today beards and long hair no longer symbolize protest. Wealthy people used to avoid the sun to show that they were members of the leisure class. Now they get suntans to indicate that they are. What is more confusing, the working class now gets suntans to look like the leisure class.

Obviously, we often need and use symbols to tell us how to react to various situations and circumstances. Roadsigns warn us about a curve or an intersection.

Roadmaps tell us how to get some place. But even the best maps have shortcomings, sometimes even mistakes. A map is not the territory. Certainly, a map is not the whole territory. A map does not contain everything that is in the territory. What is more, we can have maps of maps.

You may have heard a conversation like this:

"This can't be the road."
"Why not?"
"Because it's not on the map."

The person here identified the map with the territory. What the person may have had was an incomplete map. Your job as a writer is to draw accurate maps, maps that are clear and easy to follow, maps that measure reality with precision and care.

Look at this example of how a writer draws a map that describes how laser fusion creates energy:

> The main laser bay is in a giant clean room two stories high and nearly the size of a football field. To take the analogy a step further, a single low-power laser beam begins at one end zone, is amplified, and is divided by mirrors into six separate beams. Each beam is then amplified further and directed through one of six long tunnel-like chains of optical components. Just beyond the 50-yard line, each beam is divided again, this time into four beams, and all 24 are directed toward a four-foot stainless steel sphere right about where the opposite goal line would be.
>
> Inside the hollow sphere, all the beams converge on that single thermonuclear fuel pellet barely visible to the naked eye, and . . . pow! In that small fraction of a second, the hydrogen isotopes within the fuel pellet are fused together by an almost incredible amount of instantaneous energy—6.6 trillion watts to be exact.

It is an accurate and effective map. By using the analogy to football, the writer draws an accurate picture of the laser beam's path. To use Korzybski's metaphor, the author's verbal world stands in relation to the real world as a good map does to the territory it is supposed to represent.

But even so, the map is not the territory, and the word is not the thing. General semantics teaches us not to identify words with the things they signify. That sounds so simple, but this identification is a difficult habit to break. Not breaking it will hurt you as an observer because you will not think to ask more questions. It will hurt you as a writer because you will not be specific enough in your description and word choice.

The habit of identifying words with what they represent began way back when we began to speak. If you pointed to Bessie with a "What is that ?" look, your mother told you Bessie was a cow. If there were other cows around, you may have learned immediately an important semantic principle: Cow$_1$ is not cow$_2$ is not cow$_3$. Cows are not all alike. As a matter of fact, one cow is vastly different from any other cow. Not only does it have a different psychological framework and disposition (some cows are better natured than others), but every part of the cow is a different size and a different shape. If you were to take pictures of cows' stomachs, for example, you would find no two of them exactly alike.

Obviously, to get along at all in this world, we need to be able to identify a cow when we see one. We need, therefore, to generalize and to categorize. But it is equally important to realize that things are not what we say they are, and that one thing is not the same as another, even though we give both of them the same name.

For example, in all of this discussion about cows, you probably took for granted that we were talking about the milk cows down on the farm. Actually, any animal of which the male is called a bull has a female that is called a cow. We could have been talking about a cow moose, or a cow seal, or a cow alligator. If someone told you she saw a cow walking down Main Street, would you think to ask what kind of cow? And when you wrote your story, would you bother to indicate what kind of cow it was?

Much, of course, would depend on the context. In some stories or in some circumstances it may not be necessary to describe what kind of cow it was. The fact is, words have meanings only in context. You as the writer must always supply that context. Remember, words have no meanings; people bring meanings to words. To state it in another way, what we know is a joint product of the observer and of the observed. What we see is not what we look at; what we know is not what we know about. When we observe things and give them a name, we take them out of their context. We separate them from their environment. When we observe, we abstract; that is, we leave things out.

Usually people leave out the things they do not want to see. Sometimes they even put in things they want to see. Psychologists call this projection. You must be aware of this in your own perception of things and in the way your readers perceive what you write. Just as you see things only in the context of your own experience, so will your readers. You must provide that context, and that means that you must try to know who your readers are. Too many writers pay no attention to their audience.

Notice here how writer Jim Scott relates a scene to what is familiar to his audience:

> Suddenly, the geese rise simultaneously from the field, like a congregation at the motion of a minister's hand. They tilt their gray wings at the same angle and, sounding like a thousand schoolchildren at recess, cross the pale, blue sky.

The geese didn't rise "all at once." They didn't rise "together." They rose "like a congregation at the motion of a minister's hand." No one has trouble imagining either that or the happy, spontaneous racket of schoolchildren at recess. By comparing the sound of the geese to what we all know, Scott helps us all hear what he enjoyed hearing.

Look at how columnist Leola Floren helps us feel the anticipation of a crowd listening to the warm-up groups as it awaited Anita Bryant, the main feature of the night:

> The crowd stirs quietly, like a well-behaved child who is tolerating dinner in order to get dessert.

You can see the audience squirming in their seats. The wait is painful, almost torturous. It's all there.

Too many writers do not include that color and that context. Too many writers are content to be vague and abstract. You need to use examples, specifics, cases, data, descriptions, anecdotes, similes, metaphors. You must always be conscious of your level of abstraction.

THE ABSTRACTION LADDER

One of the prime purposes of general semantics is to make people conscious of their acts of abstracting. Every word leaves something out, even a concrete word like Bessie. But Bessie is more specific than cow, and cow is more specific than animal, and animal is more specific than organism. Semanticists say that when we get more abstract, we are climbing the abstraction ladder.

When you use words carefully, you are aware of their level of abstraction. The further down the abstraction ladder you go, the more concrete you become, and the more easily you are understood.

Notice the difference between these two statements:

> I spend a fortune each year on the food I buy for my pet.
> I spend 75 cents a day on catfood.

The second sentence has six fewer words and much more information. Note the specifics Jim Scott uses when he takes on a fox hunt:

> It is dusk in early autumn. Junior Garrett and Jim Sparks are driving along a narrow stretch of winding road between Englewood and Boydsville, pulling a trailer full of foxhounds behind a '69 Ford pickup. The narrow dirt and gravel road is rutted, and the leaves of the hickory and sycamore trees that border it are powdered by the dust raised by tractors and pickup trucks. Beyond the trees are undulating fields of soybeans and milo, stitched into squares by barbed wire fences.

The road is narrow and winding. Scott could have told us how many foxhounds were in the trailer, but he chose a different picture with a little alliteration: "a trailer full of foxhounds." He tells us "a '69 Ford pickup" was pulling the trailer, not a truck. He names the trees that are powdered by dust and how they got that way. Then he paints an exquisite picture of a quilt of moving milo. Scott is specific, concrete; he shows us rather than tells us.

Look at this dormitory scene at Ft. Leonard Wood, Mo., painted by Paula Shepard:

> Overhead lights glare off the polished, dustless barracks floors. Beds have been tucked and folded, neat as the seal of an envelope, tight as a clenched fist.

Specific, precise, graphic.

But that's not enough. You need to do more than just pile up specifics. You have to tell us what they mean. In other words, you need at times to generalize and to categorize. It is not wrong to become more abstract. On the contrary, it is necessary. Hayakawa says: "The interesting writer, the informative speaker, the accurate thinker and the sane individual operate on all levels of the abstraction ladder, moving quickly and gracefully and in orderly fashion from higher to lower, from lower to higher, with minds as lithe and deft and beautiful as monkeys in a tree."

To move gracefully and in orderly fashion up and down the abstraction ladder, the writer must first of all be aware of the process. Professor Kenneth Johnson speaks of the roller-coaster technique for writing and speaking. It involves a more-or-less systematic variation in the level of abstraction. He says if you give the reader only specific information, he may ask, "So what? What does it all add up to?" He is asking for an interpretation, a generalization. If you give only generalizations, he wants to know how you arrived at that generalization. He wants some specifics, some evidence.

In Paula Shepard's story on today's Army, for example, she moves from specifics about the living conditions in the barracks to a generalization about boot camp life.

> Today's recruits still live in open bays, but only eight, nine or 10 sleep in each. Platoon leaders and their assistants share the privilege of a smaller, separate room. Barracks are all brick now, steamheated in winter and air-conditioned in summer. And soldiers spend their dozing hours on wide, thick beds that Katt says are far more comfortable than the thinly padded folding metal cots he remembers.
> Boot camp was more rigorous all around three decades ago, he says.

The point is made. Now on to some more specifics. The insightful writer does more than look for facts and details. You must look for the inference, the judgment that gives meaning to those specifics.

REPORTS, INFERENCES, JUDGMENTS

Usually you are reporting information that can be verified. The language of reports is the language of science. Even though words mean different things to different people, we must and we do agree upon the names of certain things: inches, yards, meters, pounds. What we need is a reasonably accurate map of the territory.

Dictionaries, then, are useful maps, even though most of the time, context determines the meaning. Using a word in its most commonly accepted meaning is simply a common-sense thing to do, especially when we are writing.

For example, when Harper's Magazine called Clare Boothe Luce a "courtesan" in an article title, columnist William Safire and others took editor Michael Kingsley to task. The article was an excerpt from a book by Wilfred Sheed that contained this passage: "As a bridge-figure between the courtesan and the career girl, Clare has sometimes seemed a funny kind of feminist, and the women's movement finds her a difficult patron saint."

The most common meaning of courtesan is prostitute, a particular kind of prostitute who sells sex to the high and mighty. Kingsley told Safire that he thought a courtesan was a member of a court whose role was to serve a great rich man. "The sexual connotation is only one part of it," Kingsley said.

Safire then makes this important point about English usage: "Words not only mean what you want them to mean; words mean what they mean to most people who understand them."

He adds: "That was Lewis Carroll's satiric point, as Humpty Dumpty dismissed Alice's objection to stretching words until they lost their meaning and became sources of confusion."

The language of reports must be clear. The writer of reports, the reporter, must deal with observable data and describe them in agreed-upon terms.

An inference, on the other hand, is a statement about the unknown made on the basis of the known. We may infer that the person standing in front of a university class is a professor. We may infer that a person holding an open book in front of him knows how to read. We may infer that the dead man with the deep knife wound was murdered.

Making inferences is essential for survival. Intelligent people make intelligent inferences. What is more important, they know when they are making them. So do good writers. In addition, if they make an inference, they test its accuracy.

For example, if you were told that an employee did not receive notice that his employment had been terminated until late September, you would not write that he had been fired in late September. He did not say he was fired, and second, he did not say when he stopped working.

If you were told that it took two hours for employees of the Fire Department to put out the blaze, you would not write that firefighters put out the fire two hours after it started. You would be inferring that the employees of the Fire Department were firefighters (actually, they may have been the secretaries; the firefighters may have been on strike), and second, you don't know when the fire started.

You need to make inferences; you need to have hunches. But like a good scientist, you check them out. Far too many times we make inferences without knowing we are making them.

Look at this story:

> The musty smell of damp sawdust rises from the floor as one of 41 horses on Alice Thompson's farm stomps his feet in the chilly barn. Birds scatter from beneath the eaves when the metal doors bang open, letting in a rush of cold air.
> It seems an idyllic setting, the classic country farm.
> Yet here there is a sense of the supernatural. Here have been recorded telekinetic and extrasensory experiences for over 20 years.
> Telekinesis is the power of the mind to move objects. But it is a power many scientists doubt.

When the writer says "there is a sense of the supernatural," she has made an inference. The word itself is an inference, because no one could demonstrate scientifically that the supernatural exists.

Then the writer tells us what telekinesis *is*, and follows with a statement saying that many scientists doubt its existence. The writer confuses fact with inference.

Another story begins:

> Claude Christian is a skilled worker. He fixes cars, and he does it well.
> But Claude is unemployed.

If Claude Christian does indeed repair cars so that they run well, he could properly be called a skilled worker. But the writer is making inferences. She does not demonstrate that what she writes is true.

Now look at this carefully drawn inference in a story about the old buildings of a state mental institution:

> Bars used to surround the 3-by-7-foot pens that, during the 19th century, housed three people. There was no heat. There was no light. No beds, no toilet facilities, no cafeterias, no exercise areas—no hope.

First the writer gives concrete specifics; she demonstrates the point she's leading up to. Then comes the poignant inference—"no hope."

A judgment goes a step further than an inference. In the language of general semantics, a judgment shows approval or disapproval. A report cannot say, "It was a marvelous cruise." That is a judgment. A report would describe what the cruise cost and what specific benefits were offered.

People often make judgments when they think they are reporting facts. If you say, "Tom is a liar," you are making both an inference and a judgment. You infer that Tom often knows the truth but deliberately misrepresents it, and you make a disapproving judgment of Tom.

Many words contain or imply a judgment. They are direct expressions of approval or disapproval. For that reason these words are precarious, the most dangerous of all words. Hayakawa calls them snarl-words or purr-words. If someone says, "He always was a radical," that person is probably expressing disapproval. "She's a sweet person" expresses approval.

Look at the approval this reporter is showing in a front page news story:

> Boone County Southern District Judge Kay Roberts claimed she was new at politics, but Friday night she put on a masterful show.

By calling it a masterful show, the writer also tells us he liked what he saw. Later in the story he writes:

> Yet it was Judge Roberts who stole the spotlight.

Again he shows approval. Had he written that Judge Roberts "dominated" the discussion he would have shown disapproval.

In some writing, authors are expected to make judgments. What is important is that writers recognize when they do. When you use words that imply a favorable or unfavorable judgment, your writing is said to be slanted—and "slanted" is rarely a purr-word.

Look at these examples:

> I am firm; you are obstinate; he is bullheaded.
> We are careful with our money; they are stingy.
> I am cautious; you are timid; they are scared.
> I am slender; you are slightly thin; she is skinny.

Another word for this kind of language is that it is affective. It contains hidden emotional content. It is difficult to believe that "that mangy cur," "that lovable pup," "that silly pooch" and "that vicious animal" can all refer to the same dog, depending upon the emotional attitude of the person using the words.

Why is it that we often read that unions *demand* a pay increase, although industry *requests* or *seeks* to raise the price of its products? Here is a letter to a newspaper charging that the news media use slanted or affective language:

> In nearly every reference to the desperately needed budget cuts Reagan has proposed, the media uses words such as "axe," "chop" and "slice." With Social Security and income tax hikes, the news media have never referred to these tax increases in a similar manner. I am sure that after every tax increase every average worker feels the pain of the federal government hacking away at his take-home pay.

The writer, of course, shows his own bias, but he is not pretending to be a reporter. Here are two sentences written by a reporter in an investigative piece for a city magazine about the pornography racket:

Transactions are almost always in cash. The clientele is mostly white and mostly weird-looking.

The statements are not precise. The writer does not bother to tell us what makes someone "weird-looking." If those same people had been gathered in an art gallery or in a classroom of adults, would have they seemed "weird-looking"? Who was it that said beauty is in the eye of the beholder? The writer was not, of course, telling us *how* the people in the pornography store looked. He was telling us that he disapproved of the way they looked. And probably, he disapproved of them period.

DIRECTIVE LANGUAGE

Closely related to affective language is directive language. Directive language tries to make something happen. It tries to influence our conduct, to control future events. Sometimes directive language simply commands: "Come here!" Other times, it is more subtle: "Young ladies do not cross their legs." "All men are equal under the law."

Directive language usually contains affective language, especially in advertising and in political propaganda. Sometimes it contains a good deal of wishful thinking. "Tired of paying taxes? Vote for Jeremy Smith." The careful writer knows when to use and when to avoid directive language. You become a careful writer by learning the different uses of language.

ALLNESS OR EITHER-OR
THINKING

You must avoid, for example, the "allness" syndrome. This common syndrome occurs when you unconsciously assume that you have written all there is to say on a subject. General semanticists urge the conscious use of "etc." to indicate that you are aware that you cannot know or write everything about a subject. Obviously, you should rarely write "etc." into your copy, but you would do well to keep it in mind.

Remembering "etc." will help prevent you from using such words as *always, never, every, all, completely, every time, constantly.* The careful writer includes details and exceptions. Like the scientist, you need to look for differences, for inconsistencies. It is too easy to see similarities.

Related to "allness" is either-or thinking. Our language is loaded with polar terms because so much of life seems to be either-or: life or death, day or night, land or water, hot or cold. This also appears to be true at higher levels of abstraction: induction or deduction, materialism or idealism, capitalism or communism, Democrat or Republican.

It is perhaps natural then to think of things erroneously as black or white, good or bad, normal or abnormal. If you are not for me you are against me. The list goes on and on. "Reality" is not that simple. There are many levels of values, many shades of colors. Few things are either this or that. The scientist asks to what extent, to what degree, how much? You should train yourself to do the same. Hayakawa tells you why: "The essential feature of the multi-valued orientation is its inherent capacity to enable us to see more deeply into reality, or to appreciate its finer shadings and subtle nuances of possibilities." And if you perceive reality in this way, you can and you should find the right words to convey it to your readers.

THE NEED FOR INDEXING

One practice that may help you avoid either-or thinking and other problems of communication is what general semanticists call indexing. Again, this indexing will not actually appear in the writing, but it is a device to keep the writer conscious of necessary distinctions.

1. *The What Index.* No two things are the same. Remember, cow_1 is not cow_2 is not cow_3. Freedom of the press in the Soviet Union is not freedom of the press in the United States is not freedom of the press in Brazil. Jew_1 is not Jew_2 is not Jew_3. Labor $boss_1$ is not labor $boss_2$ is not labor $boss_3$.

You can never learn this lesson too well. Mental indexing will help you avoid stereotyping, a most common form of psychological projection. It involves a prejudgment. Some prejudgment is necessary. But the writer should be a discoverer. What is a "typical" farmer, a "typical" midwesterner, a "typical" housewife? The writer, like any other artist, sees reality freshly, differently, always for the first time.

No one is just another pretty face.

2. *The When Index.* Nor is that person with the pretty face the same day after day or even moment to moment. The only sure thing is change, and that is true of people as well as of things. Professor Max Otto wrote: "We dip an intellectual net into fluid experience and mistake a catch of abstractions for quivering life."

Not even Mt. Everest is the same as it was. The Ozarks were once higher than the Himalayas. Eldridge $Cleaver_{1982}$ is not Eldridge $Cleaver_{1972}$ is not Eldridge $Cleaver_{1962}$. You must allow for the change in things; you must allow people to change. They do.

Reporters, who primarily are chronicaling change, can never capture all the change around us. People generally want things to remain the same because that is what they are used to. But writers can help people adapt to the change around them by constantly finding it and pointing it out. After all, most things change gradually, and the change is difficult to see. But all change is easier to digest when we see it happening gradually, rather than in the form of disaster, violence or revolution.

3. *The Where Index.* Geography, climate, location have an effect on things as well as on people. Persons and things change depending on where they are at the time. A blossom on a tree is different from a blossom in a vase, is different from the blossom in a vase with water. S.I. Hayakawa in California is different from Hayakawa in Washington, D.C. Former Secretary of State Alexander Haig in a staff meeting was different from Haig in the Pentagon, was different from Haig in a Senate hearing room, is different from Haig in private life.

The what, when and where indices remind us that words are static in a world of dynamic process. The things or the people about whom you are writing continue to change, even as you write about them.

4. *Other Indices.* As with the other indices, you should remember the following when gathering information and when writing. Most of the time you are better not to say them. But your words should indicate that you are aware of them.

a. *As Far as I Know.* We always need to be reminded that it is nearly impossible to be certain about anything in this changing, moving, shifting world. Look at these statements:

> The man is not dangerous. (as far as I know)
> The gun is not loaded. (as far as I know)
> That cat does not scratch. (as far as I know)

Too many times reporters do not ask the next question or do not ask just one more person. Too many times we find the answer that we are looking for and record it as fact.

We must remember that when we describe something as "red," we do not actually know that it is red. Redness is in our heads, a joint product of our nervous system and of certain characteristics of the thing we have called red. Mostly, color is determined by the way light hits the object. Actually, the object is different colors at different times. The object would not be red under ultraviolet light, nor would a colorblind person call it red.

Remembering "as far as I know" will remind you to ask more questions and to record the answers more precisely.

b. *To a Point.* In the world outside our heads, things are true in varying degrees, at various levels, to a certain extent. The writer as scientist is always aware that what he says is true only to a limited extent. This consciousness should help you be aware that you have not said the last word on anything—because, of course, you haven't. Note these statements:

> Her clothes were out of style. (true to a point)
> He didn't need the money. (true to a point)
> She left school because she hated her math teacher. (true to a point)

A reporter wrote this sentence about the results of a new sewage disposal plant: "Neighborhoods with old facilities won't be bothered by those distinctive odors anymore." That may be true—to a point.

The truth is evasive, seldom simple, usually many-faceted. You need to demonstrate this in your writing.

c. *For Me, In My Opinion.* After all, everyone reacts to everything differently. And even that universal statement probably has some exceptions. The Latin expression is "De gustibus non est disputandum": Do not argue about taste. Remember, much of what people say is purely a matter of taste. Knowing this about others and about yourself will help you to be more precise in your reporting and writing. Read these statements:

> This is a classic example. (to me)
> The escargots had a touch too much of garlic. (for me)
> That guy was really funny. (in my opinion)

Opinion, like the inference, is legitimate and useful. Do not be afraid of opinions; just recognize them for what they are.

These are some of the ways that general semantics can help you to write what you want to write in order to mean what you want to mean. To understand words and what they do to people, you must first understand what words do to you.

Etc.

epilogue

Good writers are those who care and those who dare.

They care about people, about their readers, about their subject matter, about their work, about themselves. They take pride in what they do.

Effective writing isn't easy. Few like to write; many like to have written. After they stuff themselves with information, successful writers not only write, but they rewrite—and they rewrite. They polish, trim, sketch in a detail, create a metaphor, take one out. If, and only if, they are stuffed full of information and have worked and reworked the copy, they sometimes have moments of inspiration. Inspiration is what keeps writers writing and readers reading.

It doesn't come easily. Write a draft and then put it away for a while. When you come back to it, the real writing begins. As journalist-author Stephen Crane once told novelist Willa Cather, "The detail of a thing has to filter through my blood, and then it comes out like a native product, but it takes forever." You don't have forever, but putting away your copy for a few hours is better than for no time at all. Too often stories are in print just when the writing should begin.

You must care enough to write bright, creative copy. Again, not all subjects can be written about lightly, but you can write about them brightly. Messages, like food, can be bland or ambrosial. "If you have anything to say," director Billy Wilder advised, "wrap it in chocolate."

Ideas, after all, are entertaining. Watch the smile on a child's face at the moment of discovery, at that split second when the miracle of understanding happens. It's that "aha" moment of recognition, that sigh of intense pleasure that reassures us that communicating gives pleasure.

When communication happens, ideas we have are changed, shifted about, recreated. That's why communication is recreation, both for the writer and for the reader. The moments of inspiration and of recognition are moments of pleasure.

It's not that pleasure is the only thing to live for. It's just that people seek pleasure, and that people are at their best when they are at play. You need to work with your copy, yes, but you also need to play with it, to brighten it. Have fun with it. Good writing is a great playground; good writing gives pleasure even when the news is bad.

It's a matter of caring—and of daring. You need to be challenged and to be pushed. If there's no one around to do that, push yourself. Beginning writers on their first job often complain that no one, not even their editors, criticizes the copy. First drafts are too easily accepted, or copy is changed or deleted without any discussion with the writer. Students may find it difficult to believe, but most editors are not demanding enough. Professors won't be there to grade your work; you will have to grade yourself.

Most experienced writers, especially staff writers, tend to be energy savers. Many fall into patterns and formulas and suffer various degrees of burnout. They have been edited and cut and edited some more. They have been battered and bruised and bounced around, and they have learned to play the company game—whether that company is a newspaper, magazine, house organ or whatever. If they ever risked being creative, they have long since stopped. They tried being creative once, or a dozen times, and someone always told them they were being too cute. They tried something new, and someone stopped them, or worse, no one noticed. The fun has oozed out of their writing—for themselves and for their readers.

If any of this has happened to you, no one can help you except yourself. If you're not getting a kick out of your writing, no one else is getting pleasure from reading you.

Nothing comes from nothing. Quality writing is done by people of quality. Robert Pirsig, in *Zen and the Art of Motorcycle Maintenance*, says quality depends on three things: self-reliance, integrity and gumption. If you are self-reliant, you will not blame your boss, or your mother, or your journalism teacher for the kind of writing you do. Second, you have to like who you are and what you do. If you feel good about what you write, it will show. Third, no matter how many prizes you have won or how much criticism you have received, you have to have the gumption to give it your best, one more time. When Frank Lloyd Wright was 76, someone asked him what his best-designed building was. Without hesitation he replied, "My next one."

Make your next story your best one. And have fun.

Pages 8-9, reprinted by permission of Everett S. Allen.

Page 9, reprinted by permission of the *Gannetteer*, Rochester, N.Y.

Pages 11-12, *Scoop*, by Evelyn Waugh. Reprinted by permission of Little, Brown and Company.

Page 14, reprinted by permission of the *Village Voice*, New York, N.Y.

Page 15, reprinted by permission of the *Washington Post*.

Page 16, reprinted by permission of the *San Jose Mercury-News*.

Page 17, reprinted by permission of the *Fort Myers News-Press*.

Pages 17-18, *Scoop*, by Evelyn Waugh. Reprinted by permission of Little, Brown and Company.

Page 18, reprinted by permission of *The Wall Street Journal*, © Dow Jones & Company, Inc., 1981. All Rights Reserved.

Pages 25-31, reprinted by permission of the *Fort Lauderdale News*.

Page 32, reprinted by permission of the *Kansas City Times*, © 1981.

Page 34, reprinted by permission from the *Random House Dictionary of the English Language*, Unabridged Edition, © Copyright, 1981, by Random House, Inc.

Page 37, reprinted by permission of Corporate Report.

Page 37, reprinted by permission of Citibank.

Page 39, reprinted by permission of the *The Philadelphia Inquirer*.

Page 40, reprinted by permission of the *Seattle Times*.

Page 44, *The World of Lincoln Steffans*, edited by Ella Winter and Herbert Shapiro. Introduction by Barrows Dunham. Copyright © 1962 by Hill & Wang, Inc. Reprinted by permission of Hill & Wang.

Page 45, excerpts reprinted by permission of the *Associated Press*.

Page 46, reprinted by permission of the *Associated Press*.

Page 46, reprinted by permission of *The Philadelphia Inquirer*.

Page 46, reprinted by permission of the *Associated Press*.

Page 47, excerpts reprinted by permission of the *Associated Press*.

Page 48, reprinted by permission of the *Associated Press*.

Page 49, reprinted by permission of the *Associated Press*.

Page 49, reprinted by permission of *The Washington Post*.

Page 50, reprinted by permission of the *Nashville Tennessean*.

Page 50, excerpts reprinted by permission of the *Associated Press*.

Page 51, reprinted by permission of *United Press International*.

Page 51, © 1982 by The New York Times Company. Reprinted by permission.

Pages 74, 75, excerpts copyright 1982 Time Inc. All rights reserved. Reprinted by permission from *Time*.

Page 78, reprinted by permission of Modern Media Institute.

Page 80, reprinted by permission of the *Columbia Daily Tribune*.

Page 81, reprinted by permission of the *Detroit News*.

Page 82, reprinted by permission of the *Fort Worth Star-Telegram*.

Pages 82-83, copyright, 1981, *Los Angeles Times*. Reprinted by permission.

Page 84, excerpts are reprinted courtesy of *Sports Illustrated* from the December 21, 1981 issue. © 1981 Time Inc. "Yasser, That's My Baby" by William Nack.

Page 85, reprinted by permission of *Mother Jones* magazine.

Pages 85-86, reprinted by permission of the *Associated Press*.

Page 87, reprinted by permission of the *Philadelphia Inquirer*.

Page 88, reprinted by permission of the *Detroit News*.

Page 88, excerpts reprinted by permission of the *Kansas City Times*.

Pages 89-90, reprinted by permission of the *Kansas City Times*.

Page 90, reprinted by permission of the *Detroit News*.

Page 91, reprinted by permission of *The Miami Herald*.

Page 91, reprinted by permission of *The Wall Street Journal*, © Dow Jones & Company, Inc. 1981. All Rights Reserved.

Page 92, reprinted by permission of *The Miami Herald*.

Page 93, reprinted by permission of the *Associated Press*.

Pages 93-94, reprinted by permission of *The Philadelphia Inquirer* and David Barry.

Page 95, reprinted by permission of Becky Christiansen for Internorth.

Page 97, reprinted by permission of Don Yehle of Inland Steel Co.

Pages 97-98, reprinted by permission of the Manville Corporation.

Pages 99-100, reprinted by permission of the William Beaumont Hospital.

Page 100, reprinted by permission of General Telephone Company of Florida.

Page 100, reprinted by permission of Drohlich Associates.

Page 106, reprinted by permission of IBM Canada, Ltd.

Page 107, Mel Tansill quote reprinted by permission of Equitable Trust Bank.

Page 107, reprinted by permission of Jeanne Reinhart.

Pages 107-108, reprinted by permission of the William Beaumont Hospital.

Page 108, reprinted by permission of the Raytheon Company.

Page 109, reprinted by permission of the *Associated Press*.

Page 110, reprinted by permission of Doubleday & Company, Inc.

Page 112, reprinted by permission of the *Saturday Review Magazine* Company.

Page 113, reprinted by permission of Times Books/The New York Times Book Co., Inc. from: *Without Fear or Favor.* Copyright © 1980 by Harrison E. Salisbury.

Page 116, reprinted by permission of the *Detroit News.*

Page 120, reprinted from TWA Ambassador Magazine with permission of author and publisher; copyright 1980 by Trans World Airlines, Inc.

Page 139, *People in Quandaries*, by Wendell Johnson. Published by Harper & Row, Publishers, Inc.

Page 144, *Language in Thought and Action*, by S.I. Hayakawa. Reprinted by permission of Harcourt Brace Jovanovich, Inc. and George Allen & Unwin (Publishers) Ltd.

Page 145, from *Clare Boothe Luce* by Wilfrid Sheed. Copyright © 1982 by Wilfrid Sheed. Reprinted by permission of the publisher, E.P. Dutton, Inc.

Page 145, quotes from William Safire, © 1982 by the New York Times Company. Reprinted by permission.

Page 147, reprinted by permission of *St. Louis Globe-Democrat.*